Love and Hate
in the
Nursery and Beyond

Love and Hate
in the
Nursery and Beyond

Voices from the Unconscious

Jule Eisenbud

Frog, Ltd.
Berkeley, California

Love and Hate in the Nursery and Beyond: Voices from the Unconscious

Published by Frog, Ltd. Frog, Ltd. books are distributed by:

North Atlantic Books
P.O. Box 12327
Berkeley, California 94712

Cover illustration by Sergei Ponomarov
Cover and book design by Andrea DuFlon
Printed in the United States of America

Library of Congress Cataloging-in-Publication Data

Eisenbud, Jule
    Love and hate in the nursery and beyond : voices from the unconscious /
Jule Eisenbud.
      p. cm.
    Previously published: New York: Psyche Press, 1991.
    Includes bibliographical references (p.   ) and indexes.
    ISBN 1-883319-52-8
    1. Oedipus complex.   2. Psychoanalysis.   3. Freud, Sigmund,
1856–1939. I. Title.
[BF175.5.O33E47   1996]
150.19'52—dc20
                                 96-24594
                                     CIP

*To my daughter Joanna
but for whose gentle prodding
this book would never
have got past its gastrula stage.*

Acknowledgements

I am deeply grateful to Sara Blackburn, Professor Stephen E. Braude, Michael Harwood, and Dr. Brandt Steele for their valuable comments on all or various portions of this book.

I also wish to thank *The International Journal of Psycho-Analysis* and *The International Review of Psycho-Analysis* for permission to borrow material which ended up as parts of Chapters 2, 3, and 5. Thanks are due also to all the sources from which the reproductions used in this book were derived (see Ascriptions), and to James Lord and his publisher, Farrar, Straus and Giroux, for permission to use the lines quoted from *Giacometti: A Biography*.

Contents

Preface

In 1912 a play by George Bernard Shaw began captivating audiences with the outrageous notion that an illiterate cockney guttersnipe could be made to pass as a duchess by the simple expedient of teaching her to enunciate sentences as if she had been born to the Queen's English. Once launched, *Pygmalion,* the most universally loved of all Shaw's plays, went through numerous productions decade after decade in many languages all over the world, was made into a highly successful movie, and as the musical version, "My Fair Lady," which was also made into a widely acclaimed movie, enjoyed one of the longest theatre runs on record.

In the early summer of 1975, just in time for the surf bathing season, there took place the highly publicized release of a movie about a monstrous man-eating white shark. This "feeding machine," as it was called, had taken to mauling and swallowing bathers and just about anything else it could get into its huge maw. Within days "Jaws" broke all box office records throughout the country. At the same time it probably broke all records for keeping away from theatres the hordes of people who ordinarily flock to movies on warm summer evenings but who would not have gone to see this one, after having heard about it and seen its publicity releases, had they been paid to do so. Thus, even though the public had been informed that the Great White was only a mechanical contrivance and that no one had actually been eaten alive by it, between those who braved the movie and those whom no power on earth could have induced to do so, the depredations of the great white monster of "Jaws" terrorized about as many people as did Orson Welles' threatened Martian invasion of some years earlier.

Perhaps the last thing that would occur to a drama or movie critic is that the wide appeal of both *Pygmalion* and "Jaws" stems from much the same deep lying reservoir—or should I say cauldron—of conflicting infantile and childhood fantasies and feelings about the mother and the maternal breast, particularly the fear of their disappearance. However dissimilar the play and the movie might appear to the naked eye, the two are barely distinguishable to the naked unconscious, which perceives things through a different lens.

Both "Jaws" and *Pygmalion* attempt to cope magically, as is standard procedure in the unconscious in which both were spawned, with contradictory elements in the swirling complex of feelings around the longed for but all too often unattainable, or at least unpredictable, mother and the breast which comes to stand for her. Outstanding in this melange is the unconscious fear of one's own destructive orality on a rampage, one of the commonest psychological denominators in all culture. In "Jaws" this fear is projected outward, from whence it comes hurtling back, as in a nightmare, as a biting, tearing, unrestrainedly voracious mouth of monstrous proportions. In *Pygmalion* this fear is not manifest as such but is hidden in the latent content of the play, one of whose themes, from this point of view, is that potentially dangerous mouths can be tamed. In neither "Jaws" nor *Pygmalion,* in any case, is the theatregoer's unconscious fooled for a minute: the mouth it meets is the same, and it is his own.

This book deals with three inseparable themes centering on ambivalence to the mother. The first, the quest for the breast, is a universal striving that, as I show in my first chapter, was not only behind one of the most remarkable facets of prehistory but, in one guise or another, takes many unsuspected forms today. The second theme—also subtle in its manifestations because its real source and power reside for the most part outside of consciousness and is often seen only in its oblique manifestations —is the largely ineradicable fear of and hostility to the mother and the maternal breast. The third theme is the greatly underestimated fear of abandonment, largely as a consequence of unconscious rage against the mother. All three themes are variously woven into the tapestries of adequately functional lives, as well as those that hobble along in different degrees of misery and malfunction.

The first two themes, forever wedded to each other, make up the largest part of the universal ambivalence to women and are seen mostly in disguised form. However, the things usually associated with sublimated breast seeking—drinking, smoking, drug abuse, overeating, excessive dependency and other commonly seen derivatives of infantile orality (including, of course, the quest for the real McCoy, whether in magazines or movies given to these things or in the flesh), comprise only a few of the more easily recognizable aspects of this first, or generally more tolerable, part of the eternally divided passion that has plagued men and women as far back as the history of the sexes can be traced. Similarly, openly expressed hostility toward mothers or mother figures—or toward women in general, for that matter—is only a thin band in the total spectrum constituting the other side of the ambivalence in question, since the roster of symbolic equivalents of mothers and breasts, which can become targets by displacement for enormous amounts of murderous rage, is not easily exhausted—any more, for that matter, than is the roster of defenses against such rage. The third theme of this book, the fear of abandonment, often goes unrecognized in its manifestations. The transformations and displacements of the original fear are, however, legion.

What I propose to do in this book is expose some common denominators in different, unobvious manifestations of these important aspects of the human psyche which, like the headwaters of a many branched river, have their origin in the earliest stages of development through which even the MacDuffs among us—those who perhaps never even saw or felt a mother's or mother surrogate's bosom in their earliest years— must, with greater or lesser turmoil, pass. We shall meet artists, writers, a world renowned scientist, a celebrated naturalist, an even more celebrated philosopher, and two of movieland's greatest personages, among others. Initially, the ordinary and extraordinary activities of these persons may seem so far removed from the quiet uncomplicated pleasures of the breast, or the voracious attacks of a Great White shark, or to fears of abandonment, as to invite some question, perhaps, as to why they were included in book. But if the reader will kindly wait until all my cards have been played, these questions will, I trust, be answered, as will, in the final chapter, the question of why relations between the sexes have always been, from prehistoric times up, inescapably strained (to say the least).

Some readers may find it curious that the examples I have chosen to present are, apart from a few patients in psychotherapy or psychoanalysis, almost entirely from the ranks and works of notably creative persons. The reason for this is largely incidental. My objective is not primarily to study creativity and its mysterious springs but to explore the oftentimes devious ways of love and hate in all their variegated splendor. This can be done more efficaciously than otherwise—and more interestingly, I believe— by sending soundings into the depths of the personalities who have incorporated the drama of their childhood nightmares and struggles into their creative efforts.

Before we start, however, I should like to deal with an objection that I am certain will be raised by not a few readers, namely, that I tend to oversimplify my material in a most egregious manner. By relating many complex, variously motivated and determined behaviors and products of human thought to a few comparatively simple common denominators, it may be said, I am indulging in a style of reductionistic thinking that has long been out of historiographic fashion in these non-linear, right-brained days. The charge may be justified to some extent since to *simplify* a considerable mass of seemingly unrelated material is, as I have indicated, precisely what I propose to do. But I am not claiming a Grand Unified Theory of anything, much less of psychology and human behavior. I am perfectly well aware that determinants other than frustrated oral longings (or, on another level, the search for love), and the various positive and negative outgrowths of these after all universal aspects of the human condition, go into this or that bit of individual or group behavior, and that the fullness of life and of the people who live it can never be reduced to formula. A charge of reductionism would be justified only if I were to put forth the many surprising insights that will develop en route in this book as ultimate explanations; otherwise it would be no more to the point than if I were to show that the chemical element sodium is to be found in sea water, table salt, blood, tears, and so forth.

But let me not oversimplify the contents of this book. The ins and outs and dips and curves of the various maneuvers whereby we displace our not always admissible longings or defend ourselves against homicidal rages referable to our earliest experiences —all brought into bold relief and given a measure of coherence in terms of depth hypotheses I shall make bold to apply without further apology—are far more interesting, please believe me, than table salt. And please believe me that the cast of characters who make up the handful of people I deal with by way of illustration could have been enlarged a hundred- or a thousandfold without exhausting the richness of the human mind, the human spirit, and above all the still scandalously underestimated unconscious which presides over their manifestations.

Chapter One

The Quest for the Breast
Prehistory Revisited

In the natural state the mother-nursling relationship in mammals is regulated by a delicate interplay of sight, sound, smell, touch, taste, and still other signals that, over eons, have evolved out of what must originally have been an arrangement considerably more subject to the vagaries of chance than is the case today. In the present state of evolution, the pattern of parental care is genetically fixed in all species but man, and even here a basic underlying pattern is present beneath the individual and cultural variations that exist.

Although this kind of programming permits little scope for improvisation within a given species, the human species excepted, the range of variation between species is considerable. In some bird species, for example, the young are able to run and take care of their own nutrient needs within hours after hatching. In others, the hatchlings are helpless as they are forced to wait with beaks agape for whatever bits of food are sporadically dropped in by foraging parents. Newborn puppies, blind, deaf, and quite helpless, are ready like clockwork to begin their weaning at seven weeks, while lambs, which are up and about within minutes after birth, are nursed for at least three months. Newly foaled horses, which are able to outrun most predators within hours after birth, may nurse for a year or more.

It is a common mistake to imagine that the instinctual level of maternal care in humans is an evolutionary comedown. The contrary is more often the case. For instance, what some biologists think to be our oldest ancestor on the evolutionary ladder, the tree shrew, can only be termed an absentee parent. When the female gives birth to a litter (usually of two), she makes a nest for them sometimes at a considerable distance from the one she occupies with her lifetime consort and then checks into the nursery only about every other day. In general, the more primitive the species, the lower the level of parental care. In some species, in fact, maternal care appears to be so marginal that one can only wonder how these managed to survive the evolutionary struggle, and in other species the care of the newborn is largely paternal, as in the Emperor penguins of Antarctica, where the brooding and the care of the hatchlings is carried out entirely by the males. What is no doubt responsible for the impression that maternal care in humans is somewhat less instinctually efficient than the care that animal mothers provide is the prolonged period of infantile and juvenile dependency in humans. This provides a lot of time for a lot of things to go wrong. When they do, the results become quickly manifest.

The prolongation of immaturity in the human is thought to be the result of genetic selection pressure once the development of pair bonding, the stable family group, and the division of labor this permitted, left mothers comparatively free of the burdens of foraging and fighting, and hence with less need to get the young up and out early. The increased amount of learning through leisurely play and through group transmission of tips on staying alive that this brought about enabled the species to gain a favorable ecological niche in a field of hungry competitors. These factors also brought a vast acceleration of that purely human development, spoken language. But the storage of things learned, or culture, that this made possible within a comparatively few generations (evolutionally speaking) itself begot such a battery of things to go wrong in the now wide channel between birth and self-sufficiency that the marvel is that anything ever goes right in human development. That some things do is a triumph of nature over what is all too often, for one reason or another, less than perfect nurture.

The other purely human feature in the evolution of maternal care is the hemispherical and protuberant mammary gland. There is some question as to why such a development occurred, since other primates are as flat chested as mannequins, with only their elongated nipples offering nourishment and cheer to their highly dependent offspring. Desmond Morris, pondering the question of why breasts in his book *The Naked Ape,* concluded that the breast is less an indispensable part of the feeding apparatus than a highly effective sexual stimulus. According to him, breasts developed in humans, once they adopted the upright posture and a tendency toward face-to-face lovemaking, as a visual replacement of the buttocks which, in rear mounting primates, had originally been the releasing stimuli for copulatory and precopulatory behavior. Maybe so; but anyone who has given even passing attention to the backsides of primates will agree (I would imagine) that humans got the better of the trade. There does, in any case, happen to be a connection between breasts and buttocks quite apart from primates and their peculiar amatory preferences. This will be discussed in a later chapter. Here, if the Morris plan does not appeal to us on one ground or another, we shall have to leave unanswered the question of why breasts and return to the question of the part they play in human affairs once having arrived on the scene.

The importance of breast as breast in the human picture needs no belaboring. Mothers and children in the nursing situation have been memorialized in countless works of art, both religious and secular. Nevertheless, this seems to have been a comparatively recent cultural development, that is, within the last ten thousand years or so. In earlier times, judging from the artifacts that have survived, nursing mothers were nothing to greatly excite the artistic imagination, while children, including infants at the breast, were virtually non-existent in art (even though child burials with obvious signs of deep mourning have been found). The main objects of very early art were animals, such as can be seen in the famous cave paintings of France and Spain, and clay or stone figurines of non-nursing women, measuring from about one to several inches in length, which have been found all over Europe, from the Pyrenees to Siberia. These females, some dating back more than 30,000 years, are sometimes quite obviously pregnant, but more often they appear to be merely obese, with swollen breasts and markedly exaggerated buttocks, as seen, for example, in the 4⅛ inch high so-called Venus of Willendorf (fig. 1), named after the town of that name near the Austrian-Czech border in whose vicinity the figurine was found.

One reason for the total neglect of infants and children in paleolithic art (they do not begin to appear until the art of the Spanish Levant, perhaps 10,000 to 5,000 years ago; the Tassilian rock paintings of Africa of perhaps 4000 to 3000 BC; and Egyptian art of the third dynasty, about 2800 BC) may simply have been that more mouths were nothing greatly to celebrate when life was hard. The only thing always at a premium was food, which children as a rule were not, and it is likely that the chief objective of very early art was in one way or another to express the wish, which to the prehistoric mind was inherently imbued with magical power, that food should be plentiful. Since food consisted largely of the wandering herds of bison, reindeer, and wild horse, images of these animals plain or copulating, which signified their desired increase, or being speared by fleet-footed huntsmen, were painted or carved on rock surfaces, presumably as visual aids to magical practices aimed at insuring a steady supply of these edibles (and, of course, wearables).

The other magical technique for insuring a steady food supply may have been embodied in the Venus figurines, but not, I suspect, in the way that has conventionally been imagined. These figurines have generally been seen as signifying the idea of fertility; and in some instances this may conceivably have been the case. But this may not have been the whole story while the crucial question, in any event, would be whose fertility. The impression has often been conveyed in books on early art that it was human fertility that was intended. Nothing, in all likelihood, could be further from the truth. As has already been pointed out, children could hardly have been a primary desideratum (however much they may have been cherished once they came) when food was scarce or at best unpredictable, which could very well have been the case a good deal of the time. (We are speaking, of course, of a period before the discovery of agriculture and the domestication of livestock, when children were potential tillers and herdsmen.) In any case, it would scarcely have been warranted to expend good tribal artistry and energy on charms, incantations, and the like to bring into existence beings who, unlike the bison and the reindeer, came regularly by themselves no matter what. It makes sense to assume, thus, that pregnancy, when it was shown in the somewhat extravagantly named Venus figurines, signified the hoped for pregnancy in the animals on which man depended for his sustenance, as if such a representation might set an example for the animals to follow. This sort of thing has always and universally been a stable principle of what has been dubbed sympathetic magic.

It will naturally be asked why these primitive artists (primitive in point of time only, of course; such persons are increasingly referred to simply as preliterate) could not have gone straight to the target with representations of pregnant animals rather than of pregnant women. The fact is that they may have. Judging from the girth of some of the animals (and discounting the fact that grass eating animals often get a somewhat paunchy look when their food is plentiful), the idea of pregnancy may indeed have been intended. Nevertheless, the key to the obesity of the human female figurines may in any case lie not in their swollen abdomens but in their swollen breasts. To understand why this may be so we have to take a look at an aspect of the nursing situation that is rarely touched upon.

Associated with the sucking reflex of the newborn is the lesser known grasping reflex. This is especially strong at the time of maximum hunger, that is, when the mother, with the child in her arms, is baring her breast for feeding. The grasping and fondling of the breast which takes place at this time diminishes as satiety is reached, as do sucking movements, only to resume at the next feeding, when hunger is again at a maximum. The grasping is an integral part of the entire complex of body contact, sucking, odor, taste, warmth, and visual stimuli that makes up the nursing situation. Things are so interconnected neurophysiologically, however, that eliciting the grasping reflex will frequently result in a sucking response, and vice versa.

It is known from psychiatric and neurological studies that residues of the grasping reflex show up in adult life under stress of various kinds and may even become the basis of certain chronic symptom complexes. The reason for this has been thought to be that the neonate does not always clearly distinguish its hand from the breast and even from the mother's face, on which its eyes tend nevertheless to be intently fixed during nursing (contrary to what is shown in numerous Virgin and Child paintings which show the nursing infant Jesus gazing out at the observer of the picture). During this period, according to certain investigators, the body image is far from clear, with the infant's hand merging into the mother's breast and even her face in one primordial experiential cluster. When the breast is withdrawn (so goes the theory), continuity of the cluster is maintained by substituting the hand for the absent breast (e.g., the well-known hand and finger sucking of infants). Later on, the hand may also be substituted in the body image for the primordial face, which too is fused to some degree with the breast. Since the mother's face is frequently withdrawn at the same time as her breast, the infant's hand is left to substitute for both in the maintenance of body image and experiential continuity. Traces of this relationship may be seen in the drawings of children, in which the upper extremities grow directly out of the face, and in the behavior of the brain injured, whose hands sometimes become active in response to facial stimulation and who may come out with bizarre expressions such as "the hands of my face" and "the palm of my cheek."[1] The hand, thus, may come to be loaded with as many mnemonic associations with nursing as the mouth, so that difficulties during the nursing period may result not only in the comparatively well-known roster of oral disturbances but may also be an important root in a variety of conditions from nail biting in childhood (and later) to vascular and sensory disturbances in the hands and fingers. (I have observed the latter both as chronic and as transitory symptoms in patients undergoing analysis.) The hand-breast connection is very likely also behind the universal popularity of rubbing stones, which many persons find to have a unique tranquilizing effect. (These objects can be found from New York's Fifth Avenue and the elegant shops of London and Paris to the crowded bazaars of the Middle East and the Orient.)

To return now to the paleolithic Venus figurines. One of the best known of these is the earlier mentioned Venus of Willendorf (fig. 1) whose age has been placed somewhere around 25,000 years. It is at once apparent that this superb piece of limestone sculpture was every bit as carefully thought out and molded as the Venus de Milo. But the enormous pendulous breasts, the bulging contours of the abdomen, buttocks, thighs, and even knee pads (which are like small breasts), are very far from the classic Greek conception of the body beautiful. In fact, they give the entire figure a rather grotesque appearance if taken as a realistic representation. Symbolically, however, the Venus of Willendorf couldn't be more eloquent: with its redundant, multiple rounded contours it seems to convey nothing so much as the idea of 'breast'—indeed, of 'a breast is a breast is a breast' (so to speak).

A curious feature of the figure is its stumps of legs. These were not, contrary to a commonly held notion, the result of accidental breakage at some time in the figurine's history but of an intentionally rounded molding. It has been suggested that these stumps were meant to provide pegs by means of which the figure could be stuck in the ground. But this idea is opposed by the fact that the tips of the stumps, along with part of the body, were originally painted with red ochre, which would hardly have been a sensible thing to do in such a case.

A more plausible idea, to my mind, is that the red tipped stumps were meant to represent exactly what they must have looked like with the figurine up-ended, a pair of nipples. The fact now that the pigment *had* been partially worn off in some manner, which I discovered when I had an opportunity to hold the original figurine in my hands in Vienna's *Naturhistorisches Museum* (whose obviously nervous curator seemed anything but certain, despite my letter of introduction, that I was not some madman capable of dashing the precious piece to the ground), would be consistent with the one hypothesis toward which everything seemed to point, namely, that the Venus of Willendorf had been designed not merely to be stared at but to be held in the hand. With either the head or the leg stumps uppermost, the groove formed by the small of the figure's back and the cleavage of the buttocks provides a perfect cradle for the ball of the thumb (fig. 2). The figurine could thus have served both as a kind of rubbing stone and as a symbolic, if not actual, oral pacifier of sorts. Indeed, when one actually holds the figurine in one's hand —which from all indications is not radically different from the hand that fashioned it thousands of years ago—the impression that this groove was sculpted precisely for this purpose seems inescapable.

A number of other Venuses have been found that seem to support such a conjecture. (The total number of these figurines, well over a hundred, led Aldous Huxley to remark that for Paleolithic man every day was Mother's Day.) A Czechoslovakian Venus about 25,000 years old, 4⅜ inches in height and showing four pinpoint indentations suggestive of mammary duct openings on the top of its faceless, nipple-like head (fig. 3), has a groove in its back similar to the one of the Venus of Willendorf that fits the thumb perfectly. (Fig. 4 shows the thumb in an alternate position.) Its broken off legs, moreover, again seem as if they were intended to end in a stylized representation of some kind.

That something like this was actually in vogue across much of Europe may be seen in numerous pieces of roughly the same vintage (give or take a few thousand years) showing similar characteristics. One such is the soapstone Venus of Menton, known also as the Grimaldi Venus, found in France near the Italian border (fig. 5). Another is the astonishingly sophisticated 5¾ inch high Venus of Lespugue found in southern France (fig. 6). Carved out of ivory and abounding in rounded contours, with a faceless head and fused legs providing serviceable nipples at both ends, it is about as breasty as anything can get. (One commentator, on the very brink of insight, referred slightingly to its outsized buttocks as "two ridiculous globular masses.") A somewhat more primitive version, which could easily double as a dildo (and perhaps did—early man was nothing if not economical with his symbols and symbolic objects), is the 8⅞ inch high figurine (fig. 7) found in the north of Italy.

It is reasonable to suppose that most of these Venuses served some ritualistic purpose, possibly when used with magical incantations aimed at conjuring up visions of a plentiful food supply. The Venus of Willendorf, for example, with its built in graspability and its leg stumps serving as proxy nipples, could have expressed the hope that the hand that grasped the breast in infancy might now secure just as bountiful and satisfying sustenance by its skill in hunting. The figure might thus have afforded a kind of double-barreled magical attack on the ever-present specter of famine, while the mystical connotation of the red ochre pigment, which some think to have symbolized blood, the mother, and the sustaining earth—the very source of being for early humankind, might well have played in with this. Other figurines, even a number of crudely executed ones bearing little outward resemblance to the Willendorf prototype but which could nevertheless have been symbolically linked to it (as in the case, for instance, of the wide variety of phallic symbol forms) could have served in similar roles. Indeed, one might ask why most of these objects were sculpted in sizes that easily fitted the hand if they were not actually meant to do so.

It is tempting to conjure up a vision of a group of early humans, half of them near starvation, huddling together in caves and passing something like the well-worn Venus of Willendorf (fig. 1) from hand to hand—conceivably even from hand to mouth—while chanting sounds that in some way expressed the mystical vision outlined above. Such a picture—a prehistoric Eucharist with the Great Earth Mother in the central role—is of course entirely speculative. But it could nevertheless be substantially on track as far as early man's closeness to the unconscious springs of his own being went, and the symbolic overtones these provided. Such shapers of behavior, almost as powerful as instinct itself, might have afforded a modicum of stability in the face of the unpredictability of the life-giving herds and the dread of famine. At the same time they might have permitted an adaptive flexibility that instinct alone lacked.

Once more, however, not all Ice Age figurines were on the plump side. Indeed, some, as if sculpted by some perverse or disgruntled paleolithic Giacommeti (see Chapter 4), were deliberately fashioned as thin as rails (fig. 8) and could by no stretch of the imagination be termed "Venuses" (or even, perhaps, female). On the contrary, the symbolic duality these suggest more than hints at the ever-present ambivalence toward mother figures that clouds so much of the human psyche and human behavior. Of this, more later.

A word, finally, about the facial featurelessness which endows so many of these figurines with the vacant look of tailor's dummies. Shown in fig. 9 are two views of a Russian Venus, one of many similar figurines found on Russia's eastern plain. Its remarkable resemblance to the Venus of Willendorf indicates a widespread diffusion of what was no doubt a dominant type of stylization. That the absence of facial features was not due to any lack of skill on the part of the artist in most cases can be seen from the care with which other parts of the figures were sometimes shaped—knee pads, mons veneris, and even vaginal creases, for example. The facelessness of the figurines seems in fact to have been as deliberately contrived as their leg stumps and all around curviness.

My best guess is that this curious feature of the figurines was intended to convey something about the stage of life to which we have supposed the ritualistic use of the figurines to apply, namely, the early nursing period—and that the blank face was based upon a misconception that may turn out to underlie one of nature's best kept secrets. Paleolithic infant caregivers, in this view, may have harbored the notion, still widely held, that the newborn, although well enough able to follow the sounds and movements of the mother, were capable only of indistinct vision during the first weeks and hence were not able to differentiate facial features with any degree of clarity. The truth of the matter, as discovered only recently however, is that even two and three day old infants are capable of differential responses to the faces of mother and other caregivers and hence do not really see the mother's face as a perfectly blank wall. The origin of the mistaken notion that they do may very well lie in the lately discovered fact that since too much visual display on the part of mothers and other caregivers (pouting, sticking tongues out, and so forth) can overstimulate and disturb the infant, the latter instinctively regulates this by turning its gaze away and appearing to be unresponsive. According to some modern investigators, this simulation of 20/300 Mr. Magoo vision is a ruse of nature to prevent such overstimulation and allow other aspects of neonatal development to proceed smoothly. By about three months the ruse is dropped, however, as experiments after this time indicate that anything vaguely resembling a smooth forehead, a pair of eyes, and a nose—a mask on a coat hanger, for instance—will, if presented to the infant in full face and in motion, elicit an automatic smiling response (which nevertheless, contrary to the notions of the now delighted parents, seems to have about as much emotion connected with it as an automatic knee jerk). All the same, faceless female—and at times even male —figures that turn up in the dreams and fantasies of patients in analysis have been thought to signify the fusion of the mother's face with the smooth blank wall of the breast as perceived by the neonate. Arguable as this last notion may be, it could have fooled our early ancestors as well as countless generations of parents (and not a few analysts) with the result that featureless faces could indeed have symbolized for prehistoric humans the period of life which they intended their Venus figurines to call up.

On the other hand, early man (or woman), fashioning his (or her) figurines quite consciously to signify 'breast,' may simply (if not cynically) have considered facial features irrelevant. A curious artifact that was brought to my attention by an archeologist friend who came upon it in a collection in her charge at the Denver Museum of Natural History seems to have carried the process of dispensing with the irrelevant to its furthest point. The artifact had been discovered some years before in a burial area of the Fremont Culture Indians who, until about 1,150 AD, occupied sites in what is now the state of Utah. Labeled (for lack of better) a "concretion," the alabaster piece is the size and shape of a human female nipple and its surrounding areola. It was found near some jaw bones which could conceivably have been used ritualistically in connection with it. In figure 10 it is shown next to the nipple of a woman four days after the birth of her second child. The "nipple" of the object appears to have been worn smooth, suggesting that, in addition to its possible ceremonial use as an oral pacifier (much in the manner of the Venus figurines), it may also have been used as a rubbing stone. Here, then, would seem to be the ultimate stripped down, economy-sized version of the eternal mother and, to the newborn no-nonsense nursling, her quintessential part. The wheel had finally come full circle.

Figure 1
Venus of Willendorf

Figure 2
Graspable Venus

Figure 3
Graspable Venus

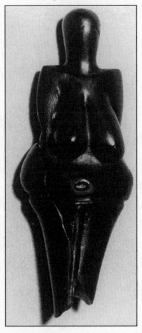

Figure 4
Graspable Venus

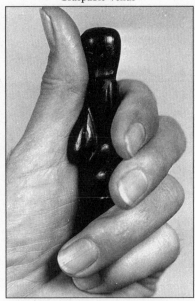

Figure 5
Venus

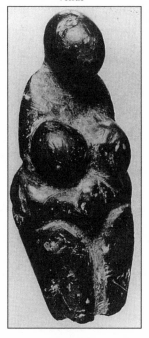

Figure 6
Venus

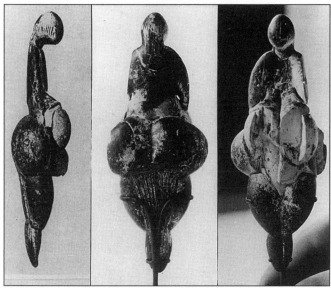

Figure 7
Venus

Figure 8
Venus

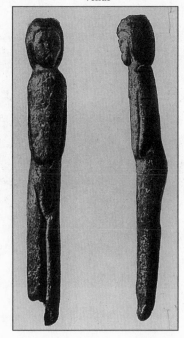

Figure 9
Venus

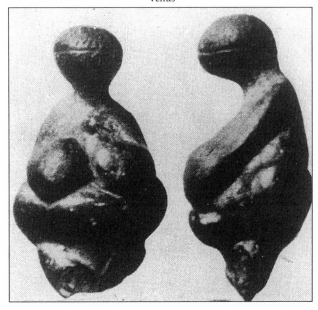

Figure 10
Fremont Culture Concretion

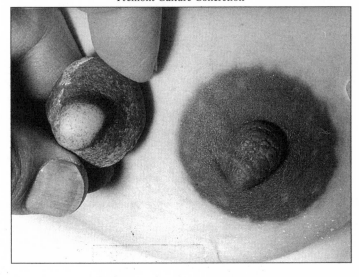

Chapter Two

The Man Who Couldn't Mourn

In most mammals early separation from the mother—even for a day—is certain death. Swift predation or less swift but just as sure starvation inevitably follow, since foundlings fare badly even within their own group. Thus the nurslings of most species may be seen hopping, ambling, trotting, wheeling, or swimming close to the mother—if indeed they are not being carried by her—as if controlled by invisible reins. But at a certain point specific for each species, something gives the signal for the process of weaning to begin. This is rarely accomplished without considerable displeasure to the young since mothers, who up to this time may have shown exceptional solicitude and tolerance, now begin to announce their change of heart (and bosom) in the plainest terms. A newly calved moose mother will turn viciously on the yearling that has had smooth suckling up to this time and will drive it aggressively away from its territory; and the gentlest bitches will snarl and snap at their pups. All this is in response to built-in timers that have finally come around to the "off" position.

With humans the story is far more complex. Heavy cultural overlays, economic factors, and enormous individual diversity may override what residues of genetic programming might still be around. What life goes on after weaning and separation from the mother rarely goes entirely smoothly. A large part of mankind spends much of its lifetime trying to crawl back to the breast or, in one way or another (as we have seen may well have been the case with the Venus figurines), trying to control and manipulate various stand-ins for the mother (and the breast), from whom (and which) it unconsciously feels most cruelly separated. Various maneuvers may also be attempted to insure that nothing that was experienced as a most painful loss could ever happen again. This, and the ins and outs and peculiar twists of the persistent inner rage that often accompanies the sequelae of separation, however brought about, is the story of a good deal of ordinary garden variety of maladjustment and unhappiness, the stuff of disordered lives and an all too often profound sense of hopelessness.

But it is also the story of a great deal that goes on in the intellectual and creative life of man. No better example of the playing out of the chaotic nightmares of childhood in these arenas exists than that of a seventeenth century French mathematician and philosopher whose lifelong need to buffer himself against any repetition of a tragic separation that cast a deadening pall over his childhood surfaced in ideas that have dominated philosophy for more than three hundred years, and quite possibly in an inspired contribution to mathematics.

René Descartes, the philosopher and mathematician in question, was born in 1596, just as the Renaissance had peaked and one of the most distinguished periods in history, the century of Newton and Shakespeare, was about to begin. His father, a lawyer and councilor in the Parlement of Rennes, was a member of the lesser nobility. Little is known about Descartes' mother except that she died in childbirth when René was fourteen months old, followed a few days later by the death of the child. The only direct reference Descartes ever made to her was towards the end of his life when he wrote in a letter to Princess Elizabeth of Bohemia, one of his numerous admirers, that she had died a few days after *his* birth "from a lung ailment brought on by some sort of distress." More than three hundred years and thousands of books and articles later this curious misstatement remains still enigmatic.

Following his mother's death, René, and an older brother and sister, were given into the charge of his maternal grandmother and a nurse. In his extensive writings and correspondence Descartes never mentioned either except for a deathbed request in a letter to his brother asking him to look after the old nurse. (There is no record of his ever having written to his sister.) When René was four, his father remarried, but little is known of his part in the child's upbringing and education beyond his referring to him as "my little philosopher" and, thirty years later, when the little philosopher had become a big philosopher, remarking that his son was "good for nothing except to be bound in calf-skin." Of the stepmother we know nothing at all.

According to his own account René was frail and sickly in early childhood, leading his doctors to despair of his surviving. Survive he did, however, and, at the age of nine or ten—rather late for French children of

station, he was sent to a royally-endowed Jesuit college, La Flèche, to begin
his formal education. Because of his delicate health, he was allowed to
spend most of his mornings in bed. This habit kept up long after he had
outgrown his childhood illnesses, however. Upon his graduation at sixteen, Descartes returned to his paternal home in Rennes where, for a while,
he passed his time in fencing, riding, and other pursuits of young country
squires with no particular drive to do anything gainful. But after some
months he wearied of this and persuaded his father to send him to Paris,
where he fell in with an indolent crowd and is said to have done some
gambling, which was about par for young men of his age and station.
Shortly thereafter, however, he abruptly disappeared for a mysterious two
year period that biographers and historians have never entirely accounted
for. The official early version is that he simply went into retreat during
this time, remaining incommunicado and not revealing his whereabouts
to anyone, including his family. A more recent version is that he spent this
period studying law in the city of Poitiers. We shall return later to this dis-
puted lacuna in the record.

The story picks up again with some certainty in 1617 with Descartes
enlisting in the peacetime Dutch army stationed at Breda, in the Province
of Brabant in The Netherlands. In 1619, however, a year after the start of
what became the disastrous Thirty Years War—perhaps the most demented
free-for-all in history, Descartes switched to the Bavarian army stationed
at Ulm. For the next two years he remained on German soil, where most
of the fighting took place, but it is unlikely that he saw any military action.
His philosophical action at Ulm, however, was considerable.

It was on one cold November night at Ulm that he had three long and
involved dreams from which, according to his own far from clear account,
he derived an almost mystical insight into philosophy and the unity of science. He also felt that his dreams revealed the path toward truth that, with
divine guidance, he would pursue from that time on. What this was all
about has remained a mystery. Generations of biographers, psychiatrists,
and psychoanalysts, including Sigmund Freud, have failed to penetrate the
almost purposely contrived veil with which Descartes shrouded this night
of illumination.

When Descartes left the Bavarian army in 1621, at all events, he is
thought already to have fashioned the major outlines of his philosophy.
Then came a seven years period of restless wandering through Europe but
in 1628, for reasons unknown, he again joined an army, this time one
besieging a Huguenot stronghold in La Rochelle, France. After a year or
so of this he took up residence in Amsterdam where, he wrote, "without

lacking any of the conveniences offered by the most populous of cities, I have been able to live as solitary and withdrawn as I would in the most remote of deserts." Amsterdam, however, was only the first of no less than two dozen cities and towns that Descartes lived in during his twenty year stay in Holland, remaining in each less than a year. This period, which has given historians no end of trouble, came to an end in 1649 when Descartes accepted the invitation of Queen Christina of Sweden to take up residence in her court. There, early in 1650, he died of pneumonia, aged 54.

So much for the bare outline of the life of an extremely complex man who, according to his own accounts, donned a mask to keep the prying world away from him. (*The Masked Philosopher* is the title of one of his biographies.) He wouldn't even let people know his birthday for fear that astrologers would get hold of it. He was particularly secretive about his whereabouts, moreover, and was given to putting false addresses on his letters to throw people off the track. Bizarrely, he even went so far as to request the recipient of one such falsely addressed letter not to reveal *its* address.

As far as is known, Descartes had only one sexual encounter in his life, but this departure from an otherwise religiously chaste life (he was a devout Catholic) occurred under circumstances that were something less than romantic. It was a one-time connection—one could hardly call it a fling, much less an affair—with a domestic servant that resulted in a child, a girl, who was promptly bundled off to another town with her mother. That Descartes was far from losing his head in this non-fling is suggested by the fact that the presumptive date of conception, carefully noted by him in the flyleaf of a notebook, happened to coincide with the period in which he was studying the physiology of gestation, a fact that has not escaped several of his biographers. The child's death at five from scarlet fever is said to have been the greatest sorrow of Descartes' life even though, from what evidence exists, he had seen little of her and there was no hint of any distress, much less grief, in his correspondence in the days imme- diately following her death. Everything about Descartes' inner life, in fact, suggests that this was the one type of thing that he had convinced himself could never—or at least should never—affect him. To understand why we have to turn to his philosophy, to what it says and what it does not say but seems plainly to mean in terms of everything we can piece together about this man who lived entirely in his thoughts.

But first, we must recognize that a philosophy, no less than a paint- ing or a poem, cannot escape its personal origins. However much it may be couched in terms of logic or rationality, it has to reflect the hidden predicates—the unconscious needs, fears, and conflicts—that characterize the psychic life and the behavior of the person who elaborates it. From this point of view Descartes' entire philosophy can be seen as a desperate effort to arrive at a rational means of escape from a dread that had haunted him since his infancy, the possibility of another loss such as that of his mother, another abandonment.

Up to comparatively recently, curiously, it was taken largely for granted that infants before the walking and talking stage were largely immune from the hopelessness and despair that follow such losses. Today, after a great deal of study, we have a better picture of such traumatic separations. Not only do infants who are subjected to the loss of mothering figures—even for days—suffer "unutterable misery," as one investigator put it,[1] but they may be sensitized for life to the real or threatened occurrence of virtually any kind of loss.

Such was the case with Descartes, but nowhere did the traces of the original trauma show themselves more clearly than in his philosophy, the major thrust of which—indeed the feature which left its imprint on all subsequent philosophy—was a denial of the key circumstance that permitted the child's vulnerability to its mother's disappearance. This, in the peculiar logic of the unconscious, was the dependency of the core of one's being, the self, on something other than the self. This, for Descartes, was the material world and what could possibly happen in it.

In his *Principles of Philosophy,* which was more or less a final draft of ideas elaborated in two earlier and in fact more widely read works, the *Discourse on Method* and the *Meditations,* Descartes wasted little time in getting to the root of the problem. He did this in two bold strokes, beginning with the necessity "to reject as false all those things as to which we can imagine the least doubt to exist." This included everything that was not self-evident. But only through the mind, the source of all knowledge, can one know what is self-evident. The mind can be deceived by the senses, however. Some malevolent demon, for example, could be putting false ideas into it. The only indubitable thing, Descartes concluded, was that he himself was there. And here the man who lived almost exclusively in his thoughts came up with a seeming truism that has never ceased to fascinate and disturb professional philosophers, the proposition that "we cannot doubt our existence without existing while we doubt." The only thing certain, he concluded, was that "I think therefore I am," his celebrated *Cogito,* from the Latin *Cogito ergo sum.*

Now, the one thing Descartes could have been virtually as certain of as the fact that he himself existed was the fact that his mother had ceased

to exist not a few days after his birth, as he stated in his letter to Elizabeth, but fourteen months later, when his attachment to her was already
profound. It was this, as indicated by his error, that Descartes must unconsciously have wanted to deny, suggesting that the problem at the root of
the pervasive doubt which came to be associated with his name was the
agonizing question, is mother going to stay put or isn't she? The answer,
implicit in everything from the *Cogito* on in Descartes' *Principles of Philosophy,* was that, insofar as Mother was a material entity bound by the
inevitable uncertainties of the material world, and since the only sure thing
was one's own self, one could never be certain.

At this point, however, comes the safety net, toward which everything
up to now in the *Principles* has been pointing: an absolute and categorical separation between the self, the "I" that thinks, and everything that
constitutes the material world—between mind and matter, in short. What
made this absolute separation between mind and matter such an effective
defense against abandonment—at least in theory—was that the funda-
mental difference between the two permitted mind to take matter (*mate-
ria* in latin) or leave it. It became a matter of election, not necessity, whether
the mind, which Descartes held to be identical with the self, need ever be
bothered by occurrences in the material world, such as a body disappearing
on you. It is the body (or matter in the generic sense) and the body only
that occupies or, as Descartes put it, is *extendable* (or conversely, by the
same token, disappearable) in space. However, the body—the *res extensa,*
the extended thing or substance—is one thing, while the mind, or "the
thing that thinks"—the *res cogitans,* which alone Descartes identifies with
the self, is quite another. *It* has nothing to do with space, and the fact of
it not being spatial renders it completely independent of whatever *is* spatial and can move—or disappear—in space.

This, then, is the hidden major premise in Descartes' philosophy, its
principal latent content which, like a magical incantation, he was to empha-
size over and over again: Material bodies (read *mater,* mother) can come
or go but "I," my essential self, my mind, my soul, my being (Descartes
was not too finicky about defining and differentiating these) remain unaf-
fected since these exist separate and apart from space and are independent of anything such as the movement of bodies in space.

This dualism, although clearly foreshadowed in Plato's philosophy,
was thereafter indelibly associated with the name of Descartes and was
indeed thenceforth referred to as Cartesian dualism—a dualism, it has
been said, from which philosophy, science, medicine, and much else have
(for better or worse) never quite recovered.

Curiously there is hardly any mention of time in Descartes' writings. This perennial mystery was just not something he was obsessed with. Matter and motion were, particularly the latter. In his *Principles* he runs on for one hundred long-winded pages about motion, which he defines as the "transference of one part of matter or one body from the vicinity of those bodies that are in immediate contact with it, and which we regard as in repose, into the vicinity of others." His discussion then becomes so convoluted and tedious that, despite one or two stunning insights (one setting forth the principle of inertia, the cornerstone of Newton's dynamics, another anticipating relativity), his English translators do not bother to provide anything beyond the headings for its different sections.

However, Descartes' peculiar obsession with motion, as we have already begun to suspect, was not confined solely to his philosophy. It showed up no less plainly in his behavior. Adrien Baillet, the seventeenth century historian and scholar, who was delegated to write Descartes' "official" biography, likened his subject's continual moving about to the wanderings of the Israelites in the Arabian desert.

When we bear in mind that Descartes' mother died at the height of his attempts to master locomotion and explore the space around him—he had no doubt already begun to play separation games with her by his tentative toddling steps away from and then his hurrying back to her—it is not too surprising that her disappearance became associated for him with the increasingly important aspects of spatial experience. In one of the three dreams he had during his night of mystical revelation while with the army at Ulm he found himself staggering and falling with every step while everyone else around him was standing upright. Whatever else this dream bit might have signified (dreams are like omnibuses in this regard: they tend to take everything they can on board), it seems so obviously to embody a reference to the "first early steps" stage of childhood as to require little further elaboration.

The question arises whether Descartes may not, in his frequent moves, have been identifying with a mother unconsciously perceived as in motion, which is the way a child who is just beginning to explore space himself might conceive of such a "going away." Such an identification might be thought of as an attempt to master the pain of the mother's disappearance with a psychological maneuver far more primitive—and, as far as it went, undoubtedly more effective—than philosophical abstraction. Something like this may have been intuitively perceived by one of Descartes' twentieth century biographers, J. R. Vrooman, when trying to comprehend Descartes' strange behavior following the loss of his child, his father, and his older sister all within a few months in 1640. "At the moment when ordinary men might have sought increased solitude and have withdrawn from society," he writes, "Descartes made another of his innumerable changes of residence and installed himself in an attractive country chateau at Endegeest." One wonders whether Descartes, whose whole philosophical defense system could have been shaken to its foundations by such massive losses, may not unconsciously have been trying to establish something like, "No one can abandon *me*; *I'll* do the moving around here." Unconscious fantasies of this kind are often behind certain dissociated mental states that masquerade merely as impulsive behavior. (It is known, for example, that sudden, seemingly inexplicable changes of locality and lifestyle, characteristically accompanied by amnesia, occur in persons who have lost important caregivers in infancy.)

Evidence that Descartes may have used personal movement for defensive purposes is suggested by other maneuvers in which he would sometimes transfer his body "from the vicinity of those bodies that were in immediate contact with it" to somewhere else. Baillet, who apparently had already sniffed something significant behind his subject's strange sudden changes of loci, tells the following story. For some time before his "flight to Holland" (as Baillet put it), Descartes had been living in Paris with some friends of his father. One day, without a word of explanation, he simply disappeared. After a month-long search his distraught host discovered him—quite by accident—living some distance away in the city. Descartes' explanation was that he merely wanted solitude. Baillet gives the story as an example of Descartes' "mania for secrecy," his *"passion pour la vie cachée."* The conjunction of secrecy and motion, however, suggests a pair of illuminating observations made by a later thinker, also something of a revolutionary, whose studies in the realm of the mind and *mater* were along lines quite different from those of Descartes.

The observations in question were made in the course of an essay by Sigmund Freud titled *Beyond the Pleasure Principle,* which had to do with the origins of the tendency to repeat one's past, the so-called repetition compulsion. They concerned a repetitive game played by an eighteen month old infant (later ascertained to be Freud's grandson). The child had a small spool that he would fling away from himself with an exclamation that seemed to signify "gone!" Then, with sounds of evident satisfaction, he would draw the spool back by means of a string attached to it. Freud concluded that the spool represented the mother, who sometimes had to leave the child for several hours, and that the game, which signified the mother's disappearance and return, enabled the child to endure these absences without crying because it provided him symbolically with a kind of active mastery of a situation he had otherwise to endure in helpless passivity. The second observation was contained in a footnote to the above in which Freud wrote: "It soon turned out, however, that during this long period of solitude the child had found a method of making *himself* disappear. He had discovered his reflection in a full length mirror which did not quite reach to the ground, so that by crouching down he could make his mirror-image 'gone'."

These simple but marvelously insightful observations have turned out to be capable of unlocking entire areas of human behavior.[2] As to the problem in hand, they suggest that Descartes' restless moving about and his passion for concealment could have had the same root in identification with the disappearing mother. By becoming himself the spool, as it were, and at the same time the disappearing image, Descartes could have been attempting actively to overcome a trauma with which he had no way of coping as a helpless infant. Such a maneuver might be thought of as somewhat akin to the sympathetic magic of preliterate tribes who imitate the animals they are hunting in order to achieve power over them.

Which brings us back to Descartes' controversial two-year disappearance during his post-adolescence and what may be one of the most clearcut instances of the concurrence of the need for secrecy and the need to "light out," as Huck Finn would have put it. The beauty of the story, as told by Baillet, is that it permits us to relate both these reactions to what is generally acknowledged to be the most significant feature of Descartes' mathematics.

According to Baillet, Descartes soon tired of playing the young-man-about-Paris in the period shortly following his graduation from La Flèche. Turning his back on his companions in indolence, he looked up a few of his former schoolmates, the most interesting of whom was a Marin Mersenne, several years his senior, who had just been ordained in the Church. Mersenne, already a mathematician of some attainments (and later one of the major intellectual activists in Europe), rekindled Descartes' interest in mathematics. But just as Descartes began to "taste the sweets" of this new relationship, as Baillet put it, Mersenne was called away to teach philosophy to young Jesuits in a town a considerable distance away, where he remained for five years. This separation, according to Baillet, affected Descartes keenly. Instead of returning to the pleasures of idleness, he wrote, Descartes withdrew completely from the world and plunged into the study of mathematics on his own in a Parisian suburb where for two years he hid from everyone.

Figure 11
"Descartes," by Frans Hals, Musée du Louvre

Figure 12
Page from *La Géométrie*

LIVRE PREMIER.   309

qui font d'vn degré plus compofées y peuuent feruir, &
ainfi a l'infini.

Au refte la premiere, & la plus fimple de toutes aprés
les fe&ions coniques, eft celle qu'on peut defcrire par
l'interfe&ion d'vne Parabole, & d'vne ligne droite, en la
façon qui fera tantoft expliquée. En forte que ie penfe
auoir entierement fatisfait a ceque Pappus nous dit auoir
efté chetché en cecy par les anciens. & ie tafcheray d'en
mettre la demonftration en peu de mots.car il m'ennuie
defia d'en tant efcrire.

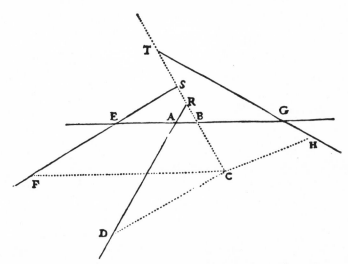

Soient AB, AD, EF, GH, &c. plufieurs lignes don-
nees par pofition, & qu'il faille trouuer vn point, comme
C, duquel ayant tiré d'autres lignes droites fur les don-
nées, comme CB, CD, CF, & CH, en forte que les
angles CBA, CDA, CFE, CHG,&c. foient donnés,
Qq 3   &

Now this story, which Baillet claimed to have obtained from a person of high position who is supposed to have got it from Descartes himself in his later years, makes eminent psychological sense. Mersenne's "disappearance," just as Descartes had begun to invest the relationship with all his adolescent yearnings for closeness and communion, was a kind of second edition of the traumatic loss Descartes had suffered in his second year of life. The feelings of desolation that must have ensued, as we know from our psychiatric and psychoanalytic studies of similar situations, could have been totally crushing had it not been for Descartes' ability to actively identify with Mersenne through the study of mathematics. This could indeed have been a life-saver not only because mathematics, like our thoughts themselves, was the realm *par excellence* that transcended the accidents of the material world, but because (as was commonly believed up to recently) it was the one realm outside of religion whose truths were steadfast and eternal. These, at least, would not suddenly vanish.

Baillet's version of the two-year historical lapse is, however, in head-on collision with a comparatively recent version that had Descartes as a law student in Poitiers during this period. This is based on the discovery that a "Renatus Descartes" was recorded as having received a baccalaureate in law at the University of Poitiers in 1616, and that the same name was on two baptismal records in the vicinity in the same year.

That Poitiers was the city Descartes' mother came from does indeed give this version a certain credibility, almost as if Descartes, at this time of terrible aloneness, had to follow some blind urge to return to his spawning ground. But outside of the names in the Poitiers registers at this time— which could quite conceivably have been of some other Renatus Descartes (after all, there have probably been other Isaac Newtons and Albert Einsteins)—nothing else supports the later version. There is not a single mention of Poitiers or its university in Descartes' extensive writings and correspondence, nor do any contemporary records or accounts besides those mentioned link him to these. On the other hand, repeated references are made by Descartes to his studies at La Flèche.

Nonetheless, if it was the person we have come to know as René Descartes the philosopher who had somehow got his name on the registers at Poitiers, there is little evidence that he had spent any amount of time in the study of law. His occasional mention of legal matters in his writings and correspondence is no more than any educated person could be expected to make, especially if from a family of lawyers. (His brother had followed his father into the law.) Even his non-mathematical writings and correspondence, on the other hand, are heavily loaded with mathematical references and material. From his chronological hints, moreover (Descartes rarely did more than hint when it came to exposing himself to historians), we can infer not only that he was intensely preoccupied with mathematics during the controversial two year gap and afterward but also that it could have been during this time that he arrived at the particular mathematical insight that came to be linked with his name.

The insight in question had to do with a method whereby any point in space can be precisely defined by giving its numerical relationship to a pair of coordinate reference lines. Descartes himself gave the (still used) terms x and y axes to these lines, while the procedures by which points in space can be specified by their numerical relationship to these lines came to constitute the beginnings of what later became known as the coordinate geometry.

Although this basic method of defining where something was in space—specifying, for example, Fifth Avenue and Forty-second Street as the place where a certain building is located—was known to the ancient Egyptians and Greeks, for whom it had practical applications in the surveying of fields and farms, a way was needed to transform numerical quantities into algebraic terms and vice versa before such a method could claim universal applicability. The beginnings of such a method go back to 11th century Persian mathematics—in fact to Omar Khayyam (he indeed of the Rubaiyat)—and were moreover being developed by other mathematicians of Descartes' time. It remained for Descartes, however, to spell out a practical method whereby numbers of lines and curves could be described in algebraic terms, and the position of every point on these lines and curves specified precisely in terms of their numerical relations to the x and y axes. The innovation introduced by this seemingly inevitable and now taken for granted departure from the geometry handed down from the time of Euclid has been hailed as one of the greatest steps in the progress of the exact sciences, the equivalent, virtually, of the transistor and the chip in applied science. The possibilities unfolding from this initial step were later refined by Descartes and others into what became the analytic geometry.[3] Which brings us to the third dimension of Descartes' lifelong preoccupation with motion; but here, in effect, the problem that was solved was, in psychological terms, that of *stopping* motion, as if he could thereby have stopped his mother, Mersenne, and others from just going off and being lost in space. The maneuvers of identifying with a body perceived to be in motion, or trying to prove that a body's materiality and motion could not affect the core of one's self and being, were fine as far as they went. But, as in the old lion tamer joke, *you* know that and *I* know that (that a well fed lion doesn't spring), but does the lion know it? What if, after all, a body *does* take off; and what if playing at being that body by identifying with it doesn't really do as much good as you thought? Then it might, as a last resort, provide at least some measure of control of a bad situation to know where that body is at any particular moment. The unconscious syllogism this time could thus have been something like what the great Joe Louis said about one of his ring opponents, "He can run, but he can't hide" (a statement not long ago appropriated by a well-known politician). Descartes, who lost no time in expanding his coordinate system to three dimensional space (whereby the trajectory of "the transference" of a body from one vicinity into another vicinity could be exactly designated) could now pin his quarry down as efficaciously as the Brown Bomber.

It should now be plain that Descartes' total preoccupation with mathematics in the period following his loss of Mersenne, and his bold use of coordinates to identify a point in space, could well have been a specific defense against the loss of loved persons, besides being, as pointed out earlier, a general defense against the inconstancy of people and circumstances. Such a maneuver would have provided Descartes, at least in his unconscious fantasy, with the utmost in magical power and control, a power and control unavailable to the unhappy infant. For the possibility of capturing in an equation the path of a moving object *is* a kind of magic: indeed, what, in a sense, can be more daringly and powerfully magical than transforming the circle, man's most ancient symbol for the breast, into a simple equation ($x^2 + y^2 = r$ being the radius of the circle) and then knowing exactly where that circle is in space? If it is imagined that something as logical and as grand as a mathematical discovery is too much to hang onto fantasies of this sort, it may be enlightening to learn that such discoveries—like a good deal else in science—have been repeatedly shown to have been ushered in by fantasies flimsier by far than these.[4]

We can now perhaps gain some understanding of Descartes' strangely erroneous version of his mother's death. Infants who are abandoned—and animals too, as experiments with monkeys have shown—often suppress all feelings of attachment to those who abandoned them. If a mother returns after an absence of weeks or months —or sometimes even days, she may find the child unaccountably cold and detached instead of overjoyed at her return. This blotting out of the mother's image is a defensive maneuver enabling the child to make the mother's absence to some degree bearable. Thus Descartes' private fiction throughout his life may have been that he had never been suckled, cradled, and caressed by a woman he could call mother, that he had, in fact, never known his mother at all.

A year before his death Descartes was to put this denial of his mother's role in his life into its most categorical form. Writing to a friend, he stated that he in no way owed his being to his parents, who were simply mechanically instrumental in his begetting. "I see no relation between the corporeal action by which I am accustomed to believe they begat me," he wrote, "and the production of a thinking substance" (which stems only from God). This just about completed his grand slam: Mother can't hurt me because, being a material object, she was never in the world of the real me to begin with; secondly, I myself can disappear whenever I please, just as she did; but she can't really disappear, thirdly, because I have a pretty clever way of always knowing exactly where she is; and besides, she wasn't my real mother in the first place.

Thus, it is hardly strange that Descartes, with this degree of armoring against loss, had the greatest difficulty in understanding anyone else's grief. To his esteemed colleague Christian Huyghens, who had just lost his wife, he sent what must surely be one of the most pathetically inappropriate condolence letters on record. "Not doubting that you govern yourself entirely by reason," he wrote, "I am convinced that it is much easier for you to console yourself ... now that there is no remedy, than it was when you still had occasion to vacillate between hope and fear. For it is certain that once hope is gone ... one no longer desires what one has lost [and] one's sorrow cannot be very painful." No recognition whatsoever by this super-thinking-substance of the fact, known to every farmhand and milkmaid who has ever suffered a bereavement, that, short of the return of the loved one, nothing could ever possibly assuage the pain of the loss. It was no doubt this sort of icy detachment that led the psychiatrist-philosopher Karl Jaspers to view Descartes with "something akin to horror."

All this armoring against loss, and these unconscious fantasies of control, turned out to be of little avail, in any case, when Descartes, the immovable object, came up against the irresistible force of the all too movable Queen Christina of Sweden. Christina, in fact, insisted that Descartes be brought to *her* for what amounted to a command performance. Against his better judgement (and deepest resistances—the child had no liking for being brought to the spool), Descartes allowed himself in the autumn of 1649 to be drafted into becoming philosopher and tutor in residence at the Snow Queen's court. If Descartes thought that Queens—mother figures *par excellence*—were supposed to stay put, he did not reckon on this one. Following two initial audiences she granted him after his arrival from a month-long journey by sea, Christina did not deign to see him again for six weeks and, for ought he could do about it, she might have disappeared behind the dark side of the moon. Then, after a brief reappearance, she took off for several weeks in the country, leaving Descartes literally cooling his heels in one of coldest Swedish winters on record.

When in January 1650 Christina finally instituted her lessons with Descartes, she insisted that they be at five in the morning, three times weekly, thus depriving him of one of the few indulgences he had ever allowed himself, his late mornings in bed. It took scarcely two weeks of this in the bitter cold before Descartes contracted pneumonia, and in a few days he was dead. One cannot help wondering to what extent Descartes' fatal pneumonia might have represented a final resigned identification with a disappearing mother when all other means of control had failed, as they so clearly had with Christina. (His mother had died, it will be recalled, of "a lung ailment brought on by some sort of distress.") And to what extent, at the same time, it might have been his final release from lifelong bondage to his internalized mother image, a problem he had no more mastered psychologically than he had philosophically. He spoke his final words on this problem, according to a friend's account, on his deathbed. "Now then, my soul, you have been captive for a long time; the hour is here when you must leave your prison, have done with the hindrance of the body." Then he added, with at last a trace of suspicion that perhaps he had not said the final word after all on the mind-body enigma, and with more than a trace of the longing for the lost mother that he had spent a lifetime denying, "You must bear this separation with joy and courage."

Thus passed the man who, for generations yet unborn, thought and therefore was, the philosopher who spent his life trying to deal with the profoundest predicate of his emotionally parched existence, the fact that the mother of his infancy suddenly was not.

Chapter Three

The Pygmalion Ploy

In recent years the trend in some circles has been to discount the long term effects of the traumata of childhood. Studies have purported to show that children who suffer the loss of important caregivers are little more at risk of developing psychological disorders in later life than any other group. But this runs so counter to clinical observation and the everyday experience of intensive psychotherapy (particularly psychoanalysis), where the effects of early losses and separations are reexperienced constantly, that one has seriously to question the methods of studies that show no counterpart to this. Consider, for instance, what happens to patients in the "perilous month of August," when psychotherapists and analysts (New York City ones anyway) customarily take their vacations. The toll of various types of regressive behaviorisms that this entails, from falling off the wagon or into strange beds to depression and a host of psychosomatic disorders, is appalling. ("New York is full of people who are crazy till Labor Day," quipped Woody Allen.) A physician patient of mine would burst into tears, as if about to lose his mummy or daddy, each time I informed him that I had to miss a session; another, in the same situation, would go on an eating binge; and a third, as if faced with an unbearable loss, would be overcome by fantasies of suicide.

The real subtleties of behavior, however, are not to be found in such obvious reactions but rather, as we saw in the last chapter, in more complex defenses against the pain of actual or threatened loss—in personality traits, intellectual styles, and creative endeavors that would not ordinarily be linked to these things.

This is not to say that all creativity is stress induced. On the contrary, most natural creativity, as seen for instance in children's play and their simple joy in exploration and the manipulation of whatever materials lie to hand, is inhibited by stress. Indeed, as the painful experiences of childhood are absorbed into the developing personality and carried over into what become makeshift ways of dealing habitually with the drab necessities and complexities of later life, natural creativity tends to be replaced by a tendency toward passive participation in the creative accomplishments of others. What enables these others to make silk purses out of the sows ears of their childhood adversities is unknown. (Certain it is that it is not simply a matter of right-brainedness or left-brainedness.) But the fact is that these magical transformations do take place and when they do it is often possible to interpret the results in terms of depth psychology. Indeed, the connection between childhood deprivation or abandonment and superior creative achievement has become a commonplace of historiography.

When it comes to dealing with the pain of abandonment, however, few persons are capable of the kind of abstract mastery of the space in which all mother surrogates must necessarily do their coming and going that the mathematically gifted Descartes was able to contrive. But other methods that people sometimes come up with can also be marvelously creative. Certainly this can be said of the inspired cry of anguish that resulted in one of the perennial favorites of the English stage, the play *Pygmalion*, whose Henry Higgins and Eliza Doolittle continue to charm audiences in every corner of the globe.

George Bernard Shaw, the impish creator of these characters, was on the surface as unlike Descartes as can be imagined. Completely the artist, mathematics was a subject he could never get the hang of even in its simpler forms (although he made a well-publicized stab at it in his later years), while wit and humor, of which Descartes could never be accused, was an integral part of his prodigious output. Shaw shared with Descartes, however, a dread of abandonment that left its mark on his entire life and work.

Shaw's mother did not die when he was an infant, but for all he knew she might have. One day she was there and the next day, and for many days thereafter, she wasn't. When Shaw was scarcely a year old and "very uneasy day and night" with his teething, according to a note in his father's diary, his mother took off for a month-long visit to her father on the other side of Ireland. The unhappy child was making his first forays into space, "plunging from nurse to me and back again to nurse," the father wrote in one of his letters to the absent mother. The "young beggar," he added, would surely be able to run down the street to meet her when she returned.

It is questionable whether Shaw would have run to meet his mother on her return even if he could have since children, following the disappearance of mothers (or mother stand-ins), tend to be most unforgiving (as pointed out in the last chapter) should these uncontrollable objects reappear. In any case, Shaw's mother, when she reappeared, was not much of a mother at all. "My family," wrote Shaw in one of his *Sixteen Self-Sketches,* "though kindly might be called loveless." What he termed "the specific maternal passion" was just not in his mother's complement of attributes. Incapable of love or hate, according to him, and wholly indifferent to his accomplishments even when he had become a celebrity, she was much more preoccupied with developing herself as a serious singer than she was with the children or her intemperate and improvident husband, from whom she eventually separated. To this end she arranged for her music coach—reputedly a cross between Svengali and Rasputin (and some think her lover)—to take up residence in her busy Dublin household, which was soon filled with trillers and boomers learning to breathe and enunciate correctly amid the continual din of pianos, harps, and assorted string and wind instruments. She was also a dedicated spiritualist, so between her singing and her seances (many of which were held in her home), and the dubious attentions of illiterate servants who, wrote Shaw, "were utterly unfit to be trusted with the charge of three cats, much less three children," the latter, of whom Shaw was the youngest, were allowed to run loose.

Shaw's mother undoubtedly subscribed to the notion, current among middle- and upper-class Victorians, that children could be entrusted to servants much as articles of clothing or packages could be left in a cloakroom, and that it didn't matter much who filled these roles so long as they knew their place and didn't steal. Unfortunately, it also didn't seem to matter how often these ill-paid daughters of the poor came and went: they were interchangeable, like shop clerks. But however unfit some of these servants may have been to take care of cats, they were often Mother to infants who knew their faces and smells and the feel of their uniformed bosoms. Thus, the sudden disappearance of these maternal stand-ins could be as much and sometimes more of an abandonment than an actual mother's disappearance. Indeed, many ill or apathetic infants may, all unbeknown to their parents, have simply been experiencing the very life being drained out of them with inarticulate grief. Thus when Shaw wrote about one of the heartless, self-indulgent replicas of his own mother who appear repeatedly in his plays and novels giving "her whole establishment the sack about once every two months," and about some child's "crying about some housemaid or other who went away,"[1] there is little doubt that he was calling upon some dimly remembered experience of his own.

Shaw early barricaded himself behind books and music, the other side of the coin that had led to his mother's neglect. (He could never remember the time he was not reading.) But when he was sixteen came the second edition (as it had with Descartes) of the abandonment he had suffered as an infant. His mother, with never a look backward, one day just picked up and followed her musical mentor to London, where she set up as a teacher of singing on her own. Left to fend for himself, Shaw tried various jobs in Dublin, such as clerking in a glove shop, but at length followed his mother to London where he lived on her bounty—and in her house—until his marriage almost three decades later. "I did not throw myself into the struggle for life," he later wrote, "I threw my mother into it."[2] Earning a grand total of six pounds in the first nine years of his London existence (five of them for writing advertisements), he cooly and confidently practiced the craft of writing that did not sell. Later he characterized himself during this period as having been "a stupendously selfish artist leaning the full weight of his hungry body on an energetic and capable woman."[3] At forty-three, after much inner turmoil, he transferred the weight of his lean and hungry body to an energetic and capable woman who happened also to be rich, and by whom he allowed himself to be captured in marriage. This millionheiress so fulfilled the role assigned to her that, by Shaw's own admission, sex never came into the picture any more than it did between Professor Henry Higgins and Eliza in a play which (as we know from a letter to the actress Ellen Terry) began to stir in his mind at just about the same time.

Pygmalion (latterly the enchanting musical *My Fair Lady*), was not actually performed until 1912. As the perfect expression of Shaw's fantasies of being able to reverse roles with the unmaternal mother of his infancy and childhood, it went on to become the most universally popular and most extensively produced of Shaw's plays. In it, instead of his suffering his mother's comings and goings in helpless desolation, as well as the many-sided oral deprivations he had to endure when she did manage to stay put (it was a matter of complete indifference to her, Shaw once wrote, what the children ate or drank, as these matters were delegated to the servants), he now fashions a Galatea whom he (via Higgins, of course) keeps a house prisoner and tortures with endless mouth exercises. The lure, not surprisingly, is always food—or chocolates or tarts—but the actuality, reflecting the deprivations and the tortures to which he had been exposed as an infant (at least this must have been his unconscious fantasy of what he once referred to as his Mother Hubbard's bare cupboard), is more often pebbles in the mouth. "If it is good enough for Demosthenes it is good enough for Eliza," cants Higgins to his straight man, Colonel Pickering.

Professor Higgins, it will be recalled, is a world-renowned expert on phonetics. The central theme of *Pygmalion* is his wager—a version of the universal fantasy of control of the errant mother—that he can train the cockney waif Eliza Doolittle to pass as a woman of class and breeding so that not even the best trained ears can detect her lowly origin. His own ears, we learn, have what amounts to absolute pitch for any voice on earth. A perfect counterpart of Descartes the geometer, he has the astonishing ability to place with exactitude, sometimes within two streets if it is London, the geographical origin—and later peregrinations—of anyone he hears speak a few words. He can do this because, being able clearly to differentiate—and play back, if needed—one hundred and thirty distinct vowel sounds, he can unfailingly place a person's dialect. The most Colonel Pickering, also a phonetics expert, can differentiate is a couple of dozen.

The highest point of dramatic tension in *Pygmalion* is reached in the final act when Eliza, who has by this time metamorphosed into an ideal mother image, and to whose voice Higgins has become irremediably accustomed, runs away. If we view the play as we would a dream and, as in the art of the interpretation of the latter, disregard its explicit chronology, this is where we would begin: with Higgins' almost unbearable anxiety at being abandoned. And this is where Higgins' expertise as a supreme phonetician comes in: no body on earth, so long as it has a mouth and can utter words, can long escape him. He finds Eliza at, of all places, his mother's house. But, confronted with her determination to not return to him (she refuses to be taken in like his housekeeper, whom he always gets around at the last minute whenever she threatens to leave), Higgins arrogantly denies his dependency in a phrase that could have come straight out of Descartes: "I can do without anybody: I have my own soul." His anxiety is finally resolved, however, by his wayward Galatea's hinted-at capitulation to the petulant and demanding infant (which is the way Shaw, with a good deal of self-insight, actually describes Higgins in his stage directions). "Oh, by the way, Eliza," he has Higgins say just before the final curtain as, with the air of a contented boa constrictor, he prepares to settle down securely with his prize, "order me a ham and a Stilton cheese, will you?"

When Shaw married his "Irish Millionairess," as he referred to her in a letter to his friends Sidney and Beatrice Webb, he made sure, in a revealing series of unconscious expressions of how things were going to be, that his bride would be pinned down in a way that Descartes or Freud's grandson—or indeed Henry Higgins—could hardly have improved upon. At the time of the wedding Shaw was suffering from a badly infected bone in his foot, and the ceremony had to be performed with him on crutches. He became further immobilized a couple of weeks later when, still incapacitated by his foot, he fractured an arm falling down a flight of stairs and had to be pushed around in a wheel chair. His new wife, he wrote to his friends, "is of course cut off from all business except my fractured limb." And in one way or another he saw to it that she was cut off from all business but him for the rest of her life. ("It seems certain to me," he wrote, "that I shall presently break all my other limbs as well.")

In a later chapter we shall see other sides of this brilliantly demanding starveling whose quest for the breast, despite the financial security and universal adulation of his later years, was unending. We shall also have a look at another psychological starveling who, although hardly so in the too, too solid flesh, and also the recipient of universal acclaim and a great deal of money, never lost his fear of ultimate abandonment. I am referring to Alfred Hitchcock, the noted master of movie suspense whose films often ingeniously expressed fantasies of pinning the mother down. The trend was clearly manifest in one of his early pictures, "The Thirty Nine Steps," where the unheroic heroine, who wants nothing more than to see the obnoxious hero get lost, finds herself literally shackled to him throughout most of the suspenseful action. The scene in which the now inseparable couple try to feed themselves while tightly handcuffed together is one of Hitchcock's master strokes. (He never missed a chance to do something revelatory of his underlying paranoia about the act of feeding.) But perhaps the ultimate defense against the threat of separation from the mother is seen in his picture "Psycho," the picture that horrified moviegoers with its frank sadism. The climax is reached when the psychotic motel keeper murderer (Anthony Perkins) turns out to be unable to differentiate himself from his ten year dead mother who, all this while, he has kept sitting in her accustomed chair in an attic room in a state of rotting mummification.

As regards being perfectly certain that Mummy is not going anywhere, Hitchcock's fantasy (it was not in the book on which the picture was based) is hard to beat. A not too distant second place, however, could have gone to a patient who had her deceased dog stuffed and mounted under glass on her mantelpiece. The dog (a bitch, of course) was the recipient of all the patient's displaced ambivalence toward her mother when alive. It was not surprising that this patient's lifelong fear of abandonment resulted in one man after another fleeing her strangulating dependency.

Another patient whose dominating fear of being abandoned quickly became intolerable to whomever he took up with (he twice attempted suicide following desertions he made inevitable) was revealed in the course of his therapy to have developed counterparts to both Cartesian and Shavian mechanisms for the magical control of space. From the beginning, an extraordinary sense of direction showed up in his dreams. In recounting them he would invariably specify the direction in which he was moving, or the position (north, south, etc.) from which he was viewing things. When I asked him how he knew this he replied that he just knew. During one session in which he pored over a map to show me where he had been for a weekend his remarkable spatial sense in waking life became apparent. He claimed never to have become lost in his travels and that, being able to backtrack on any route like a hound, he had to go through a town only once in order to be able to get from any point in it to any other point with unfailing accuracy. He was in the habit, nevertheless, of consulting his road maps constantly when driving to verify his intuitive knowledge of his position in space at any given moment. In our discussion I happened to mention that the ultimate of this kind of need to control space was seen in Shaw's Henry Higgins, whom he of course knew from *My Fair Lady*. He at once claimed that he was as good as Higgins at being able to place anyone's origin. He could unfailingly place anyone's neighborhood in the large midwestern city he was brought up in by their accent and also, he maintained, place people from just about every state in the union through their speech, although, he admitted, he was still a little weak on Minnesota and Wisconsin. I was unable to determine whether this remarkable claim had some basis in fact or was mostly fantasy, but in either case the psychological significance was clear. The patient's own speech, as if to confound any Professor Higgins he might encounter, was so slurred and muddy that I frequently had to ask him to repeat what he had just said. As part of his unconscious denial that people could get away from him, moreover, he would, when he became depressed, run up large bills, which he could ill afford, in telephone calls to distant friends, rather than to those close at hand. When I suggested that this costly habit, and much of his other behavior, added up to an early abandonment he became vehemently defensive and kept repeating, with some heat, "Oh no, not Mama" (I had not specifically mentioned "Mama") as if such an idea were unthinkable. I later learned that Mama's mysterious disappearance for a period when the patient was a year or so old was a deep and unmentionable family secret. Apparently the patient's mother had at that time left her husband without taking the children, a fact later denied by all when she adopted the role ascribed to her in the official family scenario.

Still another means of controlling space was exhibited by a wealthy bachelor in his fifties who was in the habit of importing his transient mistresses from afar, sight unseen, either from their ads placed in personal columns of different papers or from the recommendations of persons he knew in various cities. When I pointed out to him that he could do as well within a few blocks in any direction from his home in Manhattan, he acknowledged that distance added an allure that was otherwise unattainable. In the same way, he obtained a lift from whisking a woman off to the playgrounds of Europe at the very start of an affair, however casual. This exhilaration, he insisted, could not be achieved by simply going to Connecticut or Cape Cod for a weekend.

When I pointed out to this patient that his need to master space in this manner suggested some early abandonment, he too denied that any such had occurred beyond his mother having gone to a hospital for a couple of weeks when a younger sib came along. Other aspects of the patient's behavior, however, supported the presumption of something awry in his early nursing period. For one thing, he was the most dazzling malapropist I have ever encountered, even though he was well educated, a wide reader, and of superior intelligence. (A tendency toward malapropisms sometimes has roots in early oral disturbances.) Over the course of his treatment I was able to collect more than a hundred examples of his sometimes inspired neologisms. (Some of his one-liners: "She's another babble in my collection;" "A twang of conscience;" "I'm heavily ladled with fantasies;" "She asked for a salary commiserate with her abilities.") I can't really say whether I'm happy or unhappy to report that these creative gems dropped out almost entirely as the therapy progressed. The patient's undaunted attitude toward his unconventional verbalisms amounted to much the same as his attitude toward people and events. It all boiled down, as Humpty Dumpty said about words (which he insisted were to mean exactly what he intended them to mean), to the question of "Who's to be master, that's all." In using his mouth to impress his will on the world, the patient was attempting to master actively, if only symbolically, some sort of oral trauma which he must have had to suffer passively as an infant. Perhaps his mother's one absence, plus a few outwardly unremarked events during infancy (such as the sudden disappearance of a servant or sitter—experienced inwardly in oral terms) was all it took to produce a child with a damaged sense of trust in himself and others who, in later life, never seemed to know where his next meal, mistress, or million was coming from. (Perhaps not coincidentally, the patient had a definite erotic preference for servants and sitters (other people's), both in fantasy and actuality.)

Both Descartes and Shaw, as it happened, had a marked interest in the way words were spelled, pronounced, and used; and, like my malapropistic patient, both tried to impress their ideas about these subjects on a recalcitrant world. Shaw, who maintained a lifelong interest in revamping what he considered the irrational peculiarities of English spelling, left a substantial portion of his estate to a project in furtherance of this. (He preferred "cant" to "can't" and "dont" to "don't," for example.) Descartes also expressed a preference for living language and a dislike of orthographic peculiarities. He believed that if people closely followed pronunciation in their spelling it would be much easier for foreigners to learn French. In his works and correspondence, accordingly, he often used *espris* for *esprit, cors* to *corps,* and other neo-orthographisms (one of my own), much to the annoyance of his editors. In this area, thus, I strongly suspect that Descartes, Shaw, and my patient were brother infants under the skin, all having been "berift," as my globe trotting patient would say (this was one of his repeated neologisms), of good primary maternal care when they needed it.

But we have yet to exhaust the variety of stratagems pressed into service by persons who, in their creative works, unconsciously attempt to control space and the objects in it by way of mastering the pain of some early caregiver's disappearance or equivalent defection. In the next chapter we shall meet a few of the more interesting of these.

Chapter Four
The Uses of Perspective

Descartes, for all his mathematical genius, never in his wildest moments imagined that the space in which objects moved, and from which they were apt to disappear, could be anything other than the invisible box-like container, strictly up, across, and sideways, that was God given and eternal. As we know, the relativity revolution changed that picture forever. Long before Einstein, however, space was gently nudged from its Euclidean moorings (or so it was to appear) by an eighteenth century painter and engraver behind whose profound need to challenge its tyranny can again be seen the shadowy figure of a mother and her unreliable—and sometimes dangerous—breast.

William Hogarth (1697–1764), the painter and engraver of this story, is perhaps best known for his two series of satirical engravings, "The Harlot's Progress" and "The Rake's Progress." His contribution to the dismantling of Euclidean space came in a not too widely known engraving titled "False Perspective," a *detour de force* calculated to throw any right-minded viewer into confusion.

In "False Perspective" (fig. 13) objects simply do not behave as they should in the everyday world of the senses, and we are not sure but what space itself is somehow out of joint. In the lower right of the picture a well-dressed gentleman holds a fishing rod which crosses that of a villager sitting with his dog on the banks of a stream in another domain of space entirely. If we look closely, moreover, we see that the stream doesn't seem to start anywhere or go anywhere. Crossing it is a bridge whose two arches should be in the same plane but strangely do not seem to be. The one on the right is smaller, as if it were further away than the one on the left,

43

although this is plainly not the case. On the far side of the bridge (above the arches in the picture) is a sign bearing the emblem of a crescent. This object can't seem to make up its mind where it is supposed to be. It hangs from a beam anchored on a building in the middle ground, but the strut holding the beam extends from a building in the foreground, while the sign itself ends up behind some trees in the distance. On the near side of the building in the foreground, from which the strut of the beam holding the sign of the crescent proceeds, the siding seems to be going awry, as does the perspective of the paving blocks on which the gentleman in the lower right is standing: their lines diverge instead of converging (with distance), as they should. Just behind the gentleman, also, stands a barrel whose upper rim doesn't seem to know what its lower rim is doing: we look down at the former, as we should, but up at the latter, as we shouldn't. Coming back to the trees to the far side of which the sign of the crescent has mysteriously found its way, these grow larger as they recede instead of smaller. On the farthest tree, moreover, sits a bird that normally, at such a distance, would be all but invisible. Instead, it seems as large as a good-sized pterodactyl. On a distant hill, to the right of the bird in the picture, stands a Chinese who is getting a light for his pipe from a woman leaning out of the building from which the sign of the crescent is hung. Neither seems concerned with the fact, again in contradiction to the geometry of ordinary reality, that they are in arm's length contact though in two different spatial domains. At the left of the picture, finally, we see sheep moving away from us as they amble up an incline. They do not become smaller as they move into the distance but, like the trees, larger.

Hogarth's remarkable engraving is clearly a forerunner of the similarly disorienting constructions of the 20th century artist Maurits Escher, whose playful assaults on Euclid have latterly taken the fancy of the cogniscenti. But while Escher's pictures do occasionally provide glimpses into the deeper reaches of the artist's mind, none gives the insight into the psychology of perspectival manipulations—and the echoes of infantile woes—that Hogarth's unsettling creation does. What invites our attention in "False Perspective" is what we have already learned about the ways a great French Philosopher and an unhappy tot who was to become a great writer and playwright unconsciously attempted to buffer the desolating disappearances that could occur in the world of ordinary space. For even on first inspection, when we see sheep and other objects getting larger instead of smaller as they move into the distance, we can't help wondering if the unconscious message isn't once again, "Oh space, where is thy sting?" If things become larger as they move away, how can anything or anyone ever disappear?

Figure 13
Hogarth, *False Perspective*

Figure 14
Ice Age Carving

Figures 15, 16, 17
Crescents

Figure 16

Figure 17

"False Perspective," like dreams and other highly visual expressions of the unconscious, has a hidden meaning. The key to its understanding lies in the symbolic significance of the various objects and distortions of physical reality shown in it, and in the fact that among these there is a kind of common denominator that would hardly be expected if these elements were thrown together purely at random. A clue to this common denominator is suggested by the centrally located circles formed by the arches of the bridge and their reflections in the water. If we treat these as we would elements in an ordinary dream, we wouldn't have to stretch our imagination too far to see them as breast representations, which indeed circles—like any number of cognate things, such as the sun—have symbolized from earliest times. These particular breast representations, however, suggest both a fear and a denial of that fear. Insofar as they consist partly of illusions created by reflections in the water, they are only half-real, or not all there, a theme underscored in the pointedly empty barrels. The implied fear of deprivation, however, is countered by a denial of the possibility that breasts can ever really disappear. This is created by the false perspective in which the circles are drawn. The smaller of the two arches, simulating recession into the distance, remains in the same plane as the larger. It is countered also by a widely met but, considering its ancient lineage, little understood talismanic symbol, the crescent.

Like many symbols of timeless and universal appeal, the crescent seems to have acquired many meanings en route to the present (e.g., in heraldry, or as the military and religious symbol of the Ottoman Turks and Islam). Its deepest roots, however, probably derive from the feature of the moon's cyclical behavior that has been on display since long before man, its invariable return to fullness after its virtual disappearance—its death and rebirth, as it were, as in the enigmatic Ice Age rock carving shown in fig. 14. Most prehistoric crescent petroglyphs are mute in their starkness and may simply have been associated with the hoped-for return of things that had disappeared, such as life sustaining animal herds that were apt to do this for years at a time, or loved ones who had died. Crescents in various forms were sometimes buried with the latter and may also be seen on tombstones from ancient times up, as if to symbolize the resurrection of the deceased (if only into the everlasting life of the spirit). Crescent shaped knives and sickles on gravestones may have incorporated the idea of a grim reaper and at the same time the resurrection of those who were untimely reaped. Thus a more fitting symbolic summation of the graphically expressed denials of deprivation and abandonment that make up the main body of *False Perspective* could hardly have been contrived.

Of course, a lunar crescent with its horns evenly upended, as in Hogarth's engraving, is seen only in equatorial regions. Used emblematically, however, it is found in exactly the same manner on many non-equatorial tombstones, as in the Balkan Bogomil one reproduced in fig. 15, for example, where considerations of design seem to have taken precedence over astronomical precision. A similar artistic license can be seen in the use of crescents in medieval paintings and engravings of the Virgin and Child, the ultimate in security symbols (e.g., fig. 16; a modern day example is in the widely seen Virgin of Guadalupe). A down to earth version put out by the Children of God is shown in fig. 17. Here the main motif is obviously that of abundance, while the implied threat of scarcity is warded off by an amply endowed maid holding an upended crescent and in the background a fairly explicit breast form (masquerading as a mountain) standing serenely under the all nourishing sun—itself, as has been pointed out, the most ancient and universal of breast symbols.

It is not too likely that a connection between crescents and their ancient meaning was consciously entertained by the artists and craftsmen who elaborated forms of this sort. As for Hogarth (and the point of this divagation), it is likely that he too threw the crescent into his picture not because of any logical or aesthetic necessity, or because he was consciously aware of any connection between such a symbol and the other elements in the picture in one way or another centering around the threat of deprivation or abandonment, but simply because, for reasons consciously unknown to him, it just seems to have taken his "free-floating" artistic fancy.

As did, clearly, one of the most remarkable symbols of all entering into the picture's common denominator, the Chinese figure on the ambiguously situated hill. Such a figure, indeed, seems so thoroughly out of place in the bucolic English village setting of the picture (geometrical peculiarities aside) that one is inevitably led to wonder what Hogarth could possibly have had in mind in putting it there. But here again the artist's particular genius, and the creative process which became its virtually omniscient instrument, asserted itself.

Which behooves another divagation.

Long before I came across "False Perspective" I had begun to suspect that in patients' dreams, and in other expressions of the unconscious, all oriental figures—not just Chinese and, for some reason I have never understood, not only female but male figures as well—incorporated an ambivalent reference to the mother, specifically in the nursing situation. In dreams especially—and this has been encountered by other psychoanalysts as well—such figures are represented either as nurturing (serving food or drinks, for example) or as depriving or threatening (pursuing the dreamer with a crescent-shaped knife; murdering someone in a lunchroom with such a knife). Often both aspects of the early mother, her nurturing and her threatening sides, would be present, with only the life contexts in which the dreams occurred, aided by the dreamers' associations, of much use in disentangling the two.

The symbolic significance of the oriental can also be inferred from certain types of behavior. One adolescent patient, whose early nursing trauma I learned about from her severely disturbed, alcoholic, and at times violent mother, revealed that she had always longed to be an oriental. She made her eyes up to have a slanted look, possessed a sizeable collection of oriental clothes, and had acquired an extensive knowledge of Japanese and Chinese cultural, literary, and art history, as well as all sorts of trivia about Japanese and Chinese anatomy—faces, eyes, head shapes, dimensions of torsos, legs, hands, feet, and so forth. Such a degree of sublimation of an early infantile longing that had been denied satisfaction was apparently one of the few ways she could attempt to master the deprivation she had had to endure in dire helplessness as an infant. (Others were certain food rituals—counting the number of peas on her plate, for example—and a fascination with the dregs of cocktail glasses which, as a toddler, she used to go around sipping after her mother's parties.)

Ironically, this forlorn girl, who had never succeeded in pleasing her mother, would probably greatly have pleased a man whose wife, according to a UPI news item of April 18, 1962, was seeking a divorce in a Los Angeles court on the grounds that he forced her to dress, act, and cook like a Chinese to the point that her neighbors believed she actually was Chinese. She might even have pleased a "SWM" and a "DWM" (the designations for "single white male" and "divorced while male") who, in the personal columns of one 1985 issue of *The New York Review of Books,* sought liaisons with, respectively, an "Asian temptress" and an "oriental lady."[1]But who knows but what she might also have taken the fancy of a man known as the Phantom Rapist in whose possession a two-foot high oriental doll of one of his victims was found. Prominently displayed in a newspaper account of the case, this was apparently the only item he had ever taken from any of his victims.

Some years ago I presented a paper on "The Mother as Oriental" before a psychoanalytic group but decided to hold off publication of my material pending some clue as to *why* oriental figures should symbolize the mother in an ambivalently perceived nursing situation. I am still waiting for that clue, or at least for one that is more than just remotely relevant.

Symbols such as the circle can be intuitively grasped, and even the crescent can be shown to make sense. The symbol of the oriental, however, seems hopelessly esoteric and beyond our conscious reach. It may just be wired into our minds (or at least in non-oriental minds) in ways that may never be logically understood. I suspect, however, that it has to do with the eyes, which are an important part of newborn infants' recognition of facial patterns. (Despite or perhaps in addition to the evidence for the primordial experiential cluster mentioned in Chapter 1, the newborn have been shown to spend more time looking at simple line drawings of a head with the eyes in their proper place—even though they may not have the foggiest idea of what they are looking at—than at drawings with the facial features scrambled, or at drawings of blank faces.) At any rate, after years of waiting for a key to the mystery the only reasonably-fetched hypothesis I can come up with is based on the fact that infants characteristically tend to lock into their mother's gaze during nursing, and that in the foreshortened perspective with which the nursing child would then see its mother's downward-gazing eyes, these could appear somewhat slit-like. I imagine that this could be experimentally tested, but lacking that (I do not work with infants, and I have not induced anyone who does to give his or her time to such a procedure), I have to be satisfied with the coherence it gives to clinical observation. In any case, it seems to me again nothing less than a stroke of genius, pure unbuttoned, unencumbered genius, for Hogarth to have come up with this symbol so out of place except in a context such as the one conjectured to be the latent theme dealt with in "False Perspective."

As I have pointed out, however, the symbol of the oriental—at least as it shows up in dreams and other clinical circumstances—does not signify only the good, satisfying nursing mother. It frequently also carries a note of marked ambivalence, such as is clearly seen in an element in "False Perspective" which we must presume to be no more random in origin than any of those discussed earlier, namely, the man firing a gun right from the center of one of the half-illusory circles with which we began this analysis. If anything conveys the idea that all is not right in the nursing department—that there is in fact an element of danger in the breast and in what comes out of it, this does. Of this aspect of things, of central importance in the entire complex of fantasies that surround the early experience with mother and the breast, more in later chapters. It may come as something of a letdown to be told now that we have no conclusive biographical evidence supporting our conjectures about the hidden meaning of "False Perspective." Unlike Descartes' mother, Hogarth's mother, like Shaw's, lived to a ripe old age. Of Hogarth's infancy and childhood we know only that he was born in poverty, that a two year older brother—and favorite play-mate—died when William was eight (three other Hogarth children died before William was born), and that his mother had a hard time keeping the family of three surviving children together during a four year period that the father spent in debtor's prison (for a good part of which, how-ever, the family was allowed to be with him inside the prison compound).

Despite the lack of definite support for our conjecture, there are, nev-ertheless, indirect grounds in addition to "False Perspective" for suspect-ing that Hogarth may indeed have suffered some sort of a traumatic separation or abandonment in his childhood. He was, for one thing, one of the founders and, throughout his life, chief benefactors of a Foundling Hospital, established in London by Royal Charter in 1739, "for the recep-tion, maintenance and education of exposed and deserted children," for which, in consideration of "the deplorable Case of great Numbers of New-born children daily exposed to Destruction through the cruelty or poverty of their Parents,"[2] he designed a "head piece" for a Power of Attorney used for the appointment of persons to solicit funds for the hospital. The engraving shows, in addition to a number of happy foundlings already wards of the hospital, one infant just taken from a weeping mother who was apparently about to do it to death, and another (cf. fig. 13) who had been left by the side of a stream running under the arch of a bridge. (Actu-ally, the death rate of children taken into the Hospital was almost as high as that of children who were abandoned, in consideration of which Hog-arth and his wife, themselves childless, took several of the Foundling's charges into their country home outside London.)

A second item supporting the presumption of Hogarth's greater-than-average interest in abandoned children—if, indeed, not deeply felt identi-fication with them—is the well-known engraving done in 1750, four years before "False Perspective," titled "Gin Lane" (fig. 18). In this rendering of the horrors of drink we see one luckless infant carelessly being allowed to fall—perhaps fatally—by a sodden, pinch-snuffing mother, the skew-ering of another infant, a crying and presumably abandoned third infant on the ground beside the crude coffin into which its mother is being low-ered, and the substitution of gin for mother's milk in the case of a fourth. The look of horror in the face of the first infant is probably not too far from an accurate reflection of Hogarth's profound feelings about mater-nal abandonment. (This picture, incidentally, was the only one of Hoga-rth's that had stuck in the mind of my globe trotting patient of the last chapter—and he always recalled it with a shudder, he claimed, because of the look of horror on the face of the child being abandoned by the mother "with her breasts sticking out.")

Now a note for the statistically minded. Although Hogarth drew, painted, designed, and engraved scores of emblems, heraldic and other, on walls and other surfaces, and on various types of hanging shields on inns, shops, roadside poles, and in other situations, there is only one emblematic use of a crescent, other than the one in "False Perspective," to be found in two hundred and ninety four engravings reproduced in the most complete collection of *Hogarth's Graphic Works*.[3] This turns up in an engraving based upon a drawing by Hogarth for the Arms of none other than the Foundling Hospital (fig. 19). (A painted version of this engraving was placed over the doorway to the House of Governors of the Hospital.) Although the crescent was not in Hogarth's drawing, it is almost too much to believe that Hogarth did not instruct the engraver to include this symbol above the telltale cry for help from the abandoned child in the picture, especially as what a nineteenth century anecdotalist drily described as "a woman full of nipples"[4] *was* in Hogarth's drawing. Whatever the case, the constellation of elements in the engraving—especially in the "aid for poor abandoned foundlings" context for which these were assembled—points suggestively toward a latent unconscious content completely consonant with what we have already deduced to be the case in "False Perspective."

The absence of direct evidence of early nursing or other traumata related to the mother in Hogarth's case need not, then, be taken as anything more than an example of a common tendency among biographers to scant the earliest years of their subjects, or at least to view them with a high degree of psychological myopia. "False Perspective" tells its own story, and it is one which, in conjunction with what we are able to learn from other of Hogarth's works and a major theme of his adult life, leaves us plenty of lines to read between. It is not necessary to assume that Hogarth's mother drank or was a "bad" mother (although neither can be ruled out). One need only entertain something like the possibility that, although most of the time "good enough" (a term frequently used in the literature of child development), she at some point or period during William's childhood fell apart, overwhelmed perhaps by the many burdens of her miserable hand-to-mouth existence, and was, so far as the children were concerned, effactually "gone." When we remind ourselves of how often crucial details about the early lives of children who have been abandoned or otherwise traumatized come to light only by happenstance, that the "disappearance" of Shaw's mother, for example, came to light only through the father's diaries, and that the grief occasioned by the comings and goings of nursemaids in the Shaw household was revealed only in a casual remark by Shaw himself in later life, we may feel easier about pressing into service a minimal hypothesis of this kind that can at least pull us in from the cold and not leave us with a bunch of chaotic, disconnected data of no conceivable use to anyone.

Two

A curious resemblance to certain features of "False Perspective" can be seen in a drawing of a patient diagnosed in a Vienna clinic as schizophrenic and epileptic. In fig. 20 what are no doubt supposed to represent animals of some sort (however much they resemble cockroaches) can be seen to be growing larger as they move into the distance on a road that pays no attention to the rest of the landscape. Similarly, a tree on the hilly horizon is as large as one in the foreground, and an automobile in the foreground is scarcely larger than one of the animals (or cockroaches) in the distance. Only in his frankly psychotic periods, however, did the patient effect distortions of perspective of this sort; in his remission phases he drew normal appearing landscapes.

Again regrettably, no details of this patient's infancy and childhood were provided by the Viennese physician who sent me his strange drawing (which he had had engraved). Nor were any given in a later article on the case in *Science* (November 26, 1971). Again, however, I feel justified in bringing this drawing into our discussion of the long shadow cast by infantile traumata since the early histories of persons suffering from—and bravely coping as best they can with—one or another forms of the cruel illness known as schizophrenia abound in abandonments. Also common are various kinds of symptomatic denials of separation and loss, such as ideas of being in telepathic contact with people over great distances, or of being in communication with distant planets—grandiose equivalents of the Cartesian or Shavian denials of the finality of separation and loss. Frequently seen in the drawings and paintings of these patients, moreover, are blazing Van Gogh suns, such as is seen in the drawing in fig. 20 (and in the Mountin' Maid drawing shown in fig. 17), thought to represent denials of cold, insecure, breast-starved infancies (or simply, sometimes, of generally hostile and rejecting environments). All in all, thus, I am inclined to think that the intriguing correspondence between the drawings in fig. 13 and fig. 20 does not represent a purely chance coincidence.

Figure 18
Hogarth, *Gin Lane*

Figure 19
Arms for Foundling Hospital

Figure 20
Schizophrenic's Drawing

Figure 21
Munch, *The Scream*

Figure 22
Utrillo Street Scene

Figure 23
Utrillo Street Scene

Three

Mysterious are the ways of the unconscious, however, since contradictory expressions can signify the same thing and a single idea can mean two opposing things. The latter feature of human mental activity, in fact, characterizes many languages, from the ancient Egyptian hieroglyphs, where single pictorial elements were used for strong and weak, far and near, command and obey, and so forth, to our own English, where we have words like "cleave," which has two antithetical meanings, as in "cleave to" and "cleave asunder." It should not be too surprising, therefore, that an underlying dread of abandonment can be seen in marked exaggerations of normal perspectival changes with distance as well as in the reversals we have just seen. Here the sudden disappearance magically defended against in the reversals is represented in its most direct and dreaded form, as if it were something that *could* happen at any time, *whoosh*!

An electrifying example of this occurs in probably the best known painting of the Norwegian artist Edvard Munch (1863–1944), "The Scream" (fig. 21). Although many of Munch's paintings reveal his lifelong obsession with separation, loneliness, and death, none does so as plainly as this convulsion of space and color, with its frank evocation of terror and its "dizzying perspective" and "intensified rush of street and railing into depth."[5] The painting, which was preceded by several sketches and another oil, was thought at the time to have expressed Munch's reaction to his father's death when the artist was twenty-five, following which he went into a deep and lasting depression. But it is not unlikely that this event served also to reactivate memories of the deaths of a brother and sister, and especially his mother's death from tuberculosis when he was four. This last is suggested by a notation in Munch's diary referring to the circumstances in which the idea for the picture came to him. "I was walking along the road with two friends ... The sun set. I felt a tinge of melancholy. Suddenly the sky became a bloody red ... My friends walked on. I stood there, trembling with fright. And I felt a loud, unending scream piercing nature." Many people, especially children, are seized with unaccountable anxiety and sadness at sunsets, which seem to evoke the loneliness of being left by mother, especially at night. For Munch, who as infant and child was witness to his mother's bloody coughing spells, sunsets must have had a more terrifying significance. A friend recorded[6] that "For some time Munch had wanted to paint the memory of a sunset. Red as blood. No, it actually *was* coagulated blood ... He talked himself sick about that sunset and about how it filled him with great anxiety." Some years afterward

Munch told one of his patrons that at the time of this experience "he felt a great fear of open places, found it difficult to cross a street, and felt great dizziness at the slightest height"[7]. Although these symptoms can be seen in a variety of circumstances, one such may certainly be that of a remnant of an overwhelming childhood anxiety at being left behind by a dying parent.

Four

Another artist who exemplified the exaggeration of perspective and "intensified rush of street" into a rapidly receding horizon was the French painter Maurice Utrillo (1883–1955). So typical of Utrillo was the scene shown in fig. 22, that fake paintings like it, signed with his name, were said in the 1960s to be the fourth largest export industry of France. Utrillo's mother, the model and painter Suzanne Valadon, was, like Shaw's mother, more interested in her career than she was in motherhood. She gave the illegitimate Maurice into the care of her mother and, according to a friend of the family, did not see the child again until he was walking and talking. But even then Maurice saw little of his inconstant mother. Growing up in her all too flickering shadow (she had her own problems), he became a Montmartre alcoholic whom the neighborhood pranksters used to ply with absinthe, just to amuse themselves, before he was a teenager. He took up painting before his first institutionalization at eighteen but spent his life in and out of mental hospitals for his alcoholic and sometimes dangerous psychotic behavior. When his work finally caught on, his mother and his wife of a late marriage exploited him mercilessly, and he spent his last years copying himself, as many others were doing. Fig. 23 shows a fairly typical Utrillo painting in which the mother lost in infancy is recaptured. "Mother" (the breastlike dome of the church of Le Sacre Coeur) is plainly visible down the street whose perspective, in this instance, has pretty much returned to normal (much as did the remission phase sketches of the Viennese schizophrenic patient).[8]

Five

It would be unthinkable to try to generalize about the symbolic meaning of the distortions of perspective exemplified by Munch and Utrillo without including some discussion of the work of Giorgio de Chirico, a twentieth century artist many of whose paintings have become especially known for such effects, as well as for their silent, brooding, timeless quality. Let it be said at the outset, however, that it would be as presumptuous to draw major inferences from any one or several paintings of this many-sided, imaginatively and technically brilliant artist as it would be to attempt to do so in the case of any single work of Leonardo or Picasso, say—if not for the fact that the one painting of de Chirico that I shall deal with has been repeatedly singled out by critics for the almost uncanny effect it evokes. Hauntingly titled "The Mystery and Melancholy of a Street" (fig. 24), the painting shows a perspectival distortion that clearly meets the geometrical criteria we have been discussing. In this instance, however, this distortion does not give the impression of an "intensified rush" of street and building into depth but rather, despite the running girl with the hoop (thought possibly to represent a spectre of de Chirico's long dead sister), of an unhurried, almost languorous beckoning into the artist's private world of loneliness, separation, and estrangement.

"The Mystery and Melancholy of a Street," done in 1914, is one of the most powerful of a group of de Chirico's pictures sometimes referred to as his metaphysical series. In this picture we are at once alerted to the possibility of a latent content having to do with abandonment not only by the exaggerated falling off of the perspectival lines in the eerily vacant building on the left, but also by the pointedly empty trailer in the shadows suggesting, as perhaps little else as tellingly could, the idea of something or someone "gone." For the depth psychologist, moreover, for whom the dreamlike quality of the painting almost demands a watchful eye for unconsciously determined symbols, the wheels of the trailer and the running child's hoop—the circles with which the reader has already become familiar—hint at a possibly underlying oral content. (In the unconscious a wheel is never just a wheel, or a hoop a hoop.) In addition, the ambiguous shadow (of a statue?) in the middle of the deserted street ahead mysteriously insinuates the idea of objects that are not real, not warm, not really there (like the reflections in the stream of the arches in Hogarth's "False Perspective"). It is probably no accident, finally, that another painting done in 1914, which shows glimpses of the same exaggerated perspective, effected again by by receding arches, is of a railroad station, the Gare Montparnasse, and is in fact titled "The Melancholy of Departure," while a third done in that year—this time with an enigmatic, completely boarded up trailer in the middle of a deserted street bounded by an arched arcade and de Chirico's typical long, day's end shadows—is titled "The Anguish of Departure." All of these, as is true of most paintings in de Chirico's metaphysical series, exude a quality of timelessness (despite a clock in "The Melancholy of Departure") that suggests the timelessness of the unconscious (if not—to the unconscious—the timelessness of the infant nursing at the breast). What made these images surface in these

Figure 24
De Chirico, *The Mystery and Melancholy of a Street*

Figure 25
Giacometti

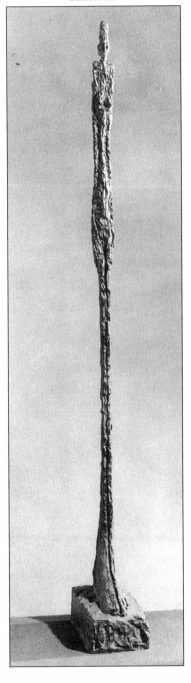

months has been a subject of some attention by critics. Probably a remark of J. T. Soby, an acknowledged authority on de Chirico, is as close to an answer as a perceptive but conventionally schooled critic might be expected to contrive. "According to legend," writes Soby in his *Georgio de Chirico* (page 72), "de Chirico at this phase of his career [after several years in Paris] was desperately homesick for Italy and thought often of returning there, only to lose hope because of the costs and complexities of the journey." It is only one step from here to the conjecture that de Chirico's homesickness and despondency called up unconscious memories of the loss of some loved one in infancy or early childhood, poignantly expressed in symbols of whose deeper meaning, that of a primal "going away" or desertion, the artist may well have been consciously unaware.

Once more, however, as in the cases of Hogarth and the young Viennese patient, definite data on anything like a traumatic childhood abandonment are lacking. No reference to anything of this sort can be found in the extensive literature on de Chirico, including his own lively and thoroughly engrossing autobiographical memoirs (unless we can take Georgio's being supplanted at the breast by a three year younger—and, it has been said, more favored—brother to be such, or his father's occasional absences on business, which would then leave the category of "abandoned child" so wide open as to be virtually meaningless). It is true that, by his own admission, de Chirico was a chronic hypochondriac who suffered, along with long spells of severe depression (the hallmark of early deprivation, genetic factors notwithstanding), a lifelong intestinal disorder, which, although accompanied by intense pain and debility, was of a presumptively functional nature (again frequently a "memory," so to speak, of infantile deprivation, if not abandonment). And it is also true that he was given to loneliness and homesickness not only for his motherland but for his thoroughly domineering mother, by whom he is thought to have felt rejected even though she followed—or at least accompanied—him wherever he went. Mostly, however, he managed to keep himself quite well in friends, enemies (sure antidotes against loneliness), and mistresses (he had one happily lasting marriage), and lived a life of outwardly expressed love and hate, no mean achievement in a member of a species given in large part to ineradicable ambivalences of a silent simmering kind. If this leaves us once more seemingly drowning in conjecture, I must nevertheless reemphasize the tendency of biographers, as well as—or perhaps especially—autobiographers, to gloss over or omit entirely the frequently unavoidable sorrows of infancy and childhood, and the abandonments, such as the desertions of nurses or housemaids who are peremptorily discharged, that take place unremarked and unremembered.

If this sounds perilously like an irrefutable, no lose position, to be eschewed in responsible argument like the plague, so be it. My first allegiance, for better or worse—and this applies also to my handling of the information gaps and ambiguities in the cases of Hogarth and the Viennese patient—is to my clinical intuition which, despite the overall coherence it provides, does not grant me the luxury of being methodologically without sin. Whether to foist my hunches on the reader is another matter; but since this is a harmless indulgence on my part, and is already in the present instance a *fait accompli* anyway, there it is, plague or no plague.

Six

Sculpture is not a medium in which marked distortions of perspective can be easily suggested. It does, however, lend itself to a procedure which can, in effect, amount to very much the same thing. While it cannot represent the external world in such a way as to give the impression of objects becoming abnormally small or large with distance, it can make objects themselves grotesquely small or large, with the rest left to the imagination (or to unconscious fantasy).

Such symbolic control of a mother whose disappearance was both dreaded and, apparently, devoutly wished was shown in some of the work of the sculptor Alberto Giacometti, a celebrated contemporary of Utrillo and de Chirico. Giacometti (1901–1966) became well known for his elongated and emaciated figurines, including female nudes whose breasts often tended to be on the perfunctory side (fig. 25). At one period in his sad, complicated, and variously bedeviled life he was dominated by a compulsion to make his figurines smaller and smaller until, when they became even smaller than pins, it became technically impossible to make them any more miniscule. He settled finally on a size that enabled him to carry several of them around in a matchbox, which he did to the amusement of some of his intimates and the ridicule of others (especially his friend Picasso). When dealers shunned his Lilliputian creations it made little difference, as did the tightening grip of a poverty that bordered on destitution. As if under a spell he could not throw off, and which he kept trying to justify in mystical terms, he kept on for months making his tiny miniatures, to the neglect of work which could at least have been traded for food.

Giacometti's relationship to his mother, who felt no sympathy for—in fact, couldn't stand—her son's craze for miniatures, was outwardly doting and reverential. But his dreams and nightmares indicated considerable unconscious fear of and hostility toward her, as did his revealing choice of subjects for his sculpture. One of these, "Woman in the form of a spider," was derived from a nightmare of a monstrous spider—in myth, legend, and psychoanalytic dream lore a symbol of the voracious, all consuming mother. With counterphobic bravado he hung this over his bed. Another of his sculptures was "Woman with her throat cut."

On the surface, Giacometti seemed to exhibit the classical oedipal split in his attitude toward women. He was impotent with those he fell in love with and sexually alive only with prostitutes, whom he made no secret of visiting regularly when he could afford to. In fact, he had his favorite whorehouse, the *Sphinx,* and even when maintaining a menage with one or another of his (under the circumstances somewhat inaptly termed) mistresses, and later during his marriage to one of them, he never tried to hide his preference in this regard. When the *Sphinx* finally had to shut its doors, Giacometti joined a good part of Paris in mourning its passing.

There was a major difference, however, between what has been classically described as the oedipally derived "madonna and the whore" syndrome and Giacometti's situation. In the former, the prostitute, though sexually alluring, is not highly esteemed, while the madonna "wife-mother," who cannot be enjoyed sexually because, in the unconscious, she belongs to a jealous and potentially castrative father, is kept on a pedestal. Giacometti put prostitutes on a pedestal and wife-mother figures, figuratively, on the street. "When I see a whore from a distance, all dressed," he said, "I see a whore. When she is in the room and naked before me, I see a goddess."[9] At the same time he often treated women with whom he became romantically involved with the sadism and insensitivity of a pimp. (This never seemed to bother them, any more than did his inability to satisfy them sexually, or his poverty.) He actually fell in love with one prostitute, a shallow, brainless creature who, with his blessing, continued to ply her trade throughout their long relationship, which ended only at his death. When his work finally caught on, and money started pouring in, he kept this woman in high style—higher, in fact, than himself. (Up to his death his shabby, unheated, delapidated Parisian studio served as his living quarters, although, with no electricity and only a rude communal facility across an open passage way for water and toilet facilities, it was little more than a hovel for which any term like "Atelier" would have been far too extravagant.) When this "goddess," true to her market place instincts, moreover, began using the pimps with whom she was still in service to extort money from Giacometti, he never complained. In fact he never ceased proclaiming, on some involved existential ground—he was a great friend of Beckett and Sartre (and this made excellent surrealist copy), that she was the only pure and awe-inspiring thing in his life.

It is difficult to see this strange—and very likely asexual—"goddess" worship, which Giacometti never disavowed to his intimates, as anything other than the equivalent, in its way, of the Black Mass, with Giacometti's austere and puritanical mother, who stood for everything his goddess of the streets was not, in the role of the Holy Mother. (His "goddess" was involved with the criminal underworld as well as in prostitution, and did a stint in prison.) There is little question but that, however Giacometti rationalized his obsession, it represented a profound psychic regurgitation of everything he had taken in with his mother's milk.

Giacometti's earliest memory of his mother was of a woman in a long black dress who excited feelings of fear and confusion in him. In later life he often could not fall asleep without first going through the repetitive fantasy of murdering and raping two women, one, 32 years of age (his mother's age when he was in his impressionable second year), in a black dress. (He also could not fall asleep in the dark—he always had to have a light burning at his bedside, or without performing the ritual of lining up his shoes and smoothed-out socks in a particular way, a type of obsessional symptom often serving unconsciously as a magical defense against an unconscious death wish.) The contradiction between Giacometti's fantasy of raping symbolic mother figures—two of them could signify, as the number 2 often does in dreams and fantasies, the two breasts—and the classical oedipal interdiction against enjoying one's mother sexually is that in the latter situation the son is too paralyzed by the unconscious fear of paternal reprisal to even dream of taking a mother figure by force. But while the inhibition of sexual interest and potency frequently has its origin in unconscious castration fears, it can also come from unconscious fears of killing one's mother through uncontrollable rage, a rage that most often is derived from deprivation of one sort or another during the earliest months and years.

We know little of this period in Giacometti's life except that he was weaned at 6 months, nothing to excite comment today but something for which there had to be a pressing reason in Alberto's ethnically conventional family. The pressing reason in this instance was the mother's pregnancy with Alberto's younger brother who, it seems, became sick on her pre-empted milk anyway. But we do know that the mother, despite Giacometti's lifelong, publicly declared devotion to her—she died at 93 when he was 62—had a domineering, critical side to her ("You'd never win a beauty contest," she once told him) and was penurious to a point of privation. (She would sit in the dark when alone to save on electricity). Her penny pinching nature, revealing a side of herself that could very well have

had its counterpart in her treatment of her son in his earliest days, came
to the fore on one (and possibly the only) occasion that the latter turned
to her for much needed financial aid. Although she had been left moder-
ately well off by her husband, Giacometti's father, a Swiss painter and art
teacher of some renown in his day, though strictly academic and light years
from any artistic greatness, she turned him down flat. Judging from a
revealing incident which occurred some time later, Giacometti may well
have identified with this side of his mother, certainly in his treatment of
the non-professional women in his life. In a scene that took place between
him and his then current hovel-mate, a live-in "mistress" and model whom
he later married, it is Giacometti himself who is seen in the role of mean,
penny pinching depriver. The setting, moreover, points suggestively to the
infantile origin of this trait in him. The victim in this turnaround of the
scene with the mother had already been living with Giacometti for some
time and worked as a part time secretary to help make ends meet. Often,
however, they simply didn't. "There were nights," writes James Lord, Giacometti's most recent and most authoritative biographer, "when they had
nothing to eat but bread and Camembert cheese. At other times Alberto
would go off by himself to dine with friends, leaving Annette to shift for
herself. On one such occasion ... Annette appeared [at the Cafe de Flore]
and said that she hadn't enough money for dinner. He told her to borrow
it, naming a possible lender, but she had already tried that person, where-
upon he named another, whom, as it turned out, she had already tried. At
this Alberto irritably said, 'Well, I'm going to have dinner with my cousins,
and I can't do anything about it now.' Chagrined, Annette turned away,
half in tears, and went off alone."[10] (When Giacometti's fortunes changed
and he took up with his awe-inspiring prostitute, Annette still came last.)

There is little question that Giacometti was in the grip of two major
neurotic developments, sometimes confluent and sometimes not, like the
two bands playing different pieces of music simultaneously in Charles Ives'
marvelous orchestral work celebrating the 4th of July. Obviously, he was
possessed by deep conflicts on the sexual level, the syndrome that psychiatric students of his life and work would probably seize upon first. As if
aware of this—and who can say he was not in that heyday of Freudian-
ism?—he fashioned his figurines, right down to the tiniest of his tiny ones,
with lumpish, swollen feet (as shown in fig. 25) which, as the father of
psychoanalysis had occasion to point out, the name "Oedipus" signified
in Greek. (Giacometti had a marked foot fetish both with women and, it
will be recalled, in his pre-sleep ritual of the socks and shoes.) Underneath
this oedipal overlay, however, resided the developmentally earlier source

of conflict about the loved and hated mother whom, as indicated by his pre-sleep fantasies and his dreams, he must often have wished dead. His emotional dependence on her, however, made dispensing with her—or leaving her—impossible. In fact the more his rage against his mother pressed toward the surface, the more he would be overcome by a dread of losing her.[11] It was for this reason that he always had to have in tow some woman whom he was able to induce to play a sexless, motherly role toward him, and upon whom, in one fashion or another, he was able to vent the unconscious hatred surging up in him, as in the Annette incident related above.

The ultimate in such ambivalence—in effect a transformation of the game played by Freud's grandson (Chapter 2) that symbolically provided him some mastery of an otherwise hopeless catch-22 conflict, was his shrinking figurines. Here, although he was apparently not in control of his compulsion to create these tiny figurines, which he tried to justify in ineffable, mystical terms (nothing new in the art world), the compulsion itself unconsciously provided a kind of magical control of the comings and goings of the mother. By means of it he was able to bring her near to extinction (some of his miniscule pin-sized figurines just fell apart like ashes when he could go no further with them) but also bring her back by his own efforts and at his own time. Meanwhile he could behave like a child who fingers the coin in his pocket with the comforting feeling that he can take it out and look at it—or spend it—any time he wishes, or like the hosts of people who have related feelings (although not always consciously thought of as such) in regard to their rubbing stones.

So, fundamentally, when translated into the language and logic of the unconscious, Giacometti's strange Alice-in-Wonderland game followed in the tradition of Descartes, Shaw, Hogarth, and others who used different means to make things disappear and to bring them back (or make them *un*disappear, as it were), to symbolically—and in the unconscious quite magically, of course—control the comings and goings of unpredictable or otherwise wayward maternal figures.

When his mother actually disappeared for the last time, Giacometti's system seemed to collapse. His game was over. The only means left to him to keep control of the mother who must never completely disappear was to become her, much as did the psychopathic breast-slasher of Alfred Hitchcock's *Psycho*. To his wife's consternation—she thought he had gone mad—he went around shouting, "Alberto, come eat! Alberto, come eat!" Three years later Alberto went to his final repast with his mother. He brought his beloved figurines to the hospital in which he spent his last days. "Soon again I will see my mother," he murmured to his doctor. At his bedside when he slipped into his final coma was, much to the chagrin of his wife and others of his family, his faithful (after her fashion) Madonna of the streets.

Seven

A final example of a work incorporating both primal separation anxiety and its denial may be seen in "Locating the Vanishing Point," (fig. 26) from *Great Moments in Architecture* by the brilliant and versatile artist David Macaulay. The latent content of this extravaganza has obvious points of similarity to that of Giacometti's compulsion to bring his miniatures to the verge of extinction. But here we are aided in our interpretation by an intriguing bit of internal evidence. What it is that is feared to be in danger of vanishing is suggested in the peculiarly symmetrical nipple-like outcroppings on the horizon. However, the idea of converging lines that never make it to the horizon implies that nothing can ever really vanish, and is thus in the tradition of the great denial maneuvers we have already encountered. Finally, both sides of the equation, the denial and the fear behind it, are seen in the couple from a time gone by walking pleasantly hand-in-hand in the middleground, suggesting the closeness and security of childhood, not otherwise present, however, in the bleak, arid, hostile landscape, where even the sky seems empty of birds—to great numbers of people the ultimate in desolation. But this deserves a chapter in itself.

Figure 26
Macaulay, *Locating the Vanishing Point*

Chapter Five

The Avian Connection

It may come as a surprise to many that the outdoor sport drawing the largest weekend numbers is not tennis or golf (or skiing) but bird-watching, which has been termed a kind of madness which can be cured only by rising at dawn and sitting in a bog. It has been estimated that there are ten million bird-watchers of various grades in the United States alone. Between Britain and America about one hundred bird books are published every year, and binocular manufacturers have reported that most of their instruments are sold not to hunters, or to racing or football fans, but to birders.

The literature of ornithology is enormous, ranging from the most insipid trash to some of the finest poetry and prose in every language. Nearly all of it, in a sense, has been addressed to the problem of the bird's enigmatic appeal. Just about everything one ordinarily associates with birds has been written about extensively in this connection: their seeming joyousness and freedom, the mysteriousness of their ways, the beauty of their form, color, and song (which last, simply an assertion of territorial rights, has inspired rhapsodic paeons few musicians have enjoyed). Probably upward of a million items have been published on bird migration alone.

No one has been satisfied that an answer has been found to the bird's mysterious appeal; but then no one, among generations of amateur and professional ornithologists—including some of the most illustrious names in science, seems ever to have perceived anything of significance in the fact that, from earliest times, one of the bird's most enduring symbolic linkages has been to the mother and the maternal breast. This is the more remarkable in that mother birds dropping bits of nourishment into the gaping beaks of their young have been a common sight, presumably, as long as hominids have been around to witness it.

Perhaps the earliest artifacts indicating a symbolic connection between the bird and the breast are a group of six remarkably similar figurines found in Russia and dated roughly at about 15,000–20,000 years ago. Fashioned from mammoth ivory and running around three-and-one-half inches in length (fig. 27), they have been taken solely as bird effigies. But it is difficult for an observer not mired in archeological detail to miss seeing them—or at least their forward parts—as breasts. They also handle easily. Each of the three specimens in my possession (casts by courtesy of the State Historical Museum in Moscow, whose curator sent them to me— unsolicited and without a covering note—after I had clued him into what seemed to me obvious), has two grooves, one on the underside of the body and the other on the topside of the tail. One's thumb fits so naturally into these (fig. 28) as inescapably to suggest that the objects may have been used in ritualistic ways similar to what may have been the case with the Venus figurines of Chapter 1. They could certainly have made serviceable oral pacifiers.

That the symbolic bird-breast connection was more than just a passing artistic whim is indicated in a startling find, dated at about 6500 BC, made a quarter of a century ago in one wall of a shrine dedicated to a reigning Anatolian Mother Goddess. Sculpted into the wall is a pair of large breasts, "elongated as if heavy with milk and meant to nourish,"[1] through whose open nipples protrude the beaks of vultures. (A vulture, plus the qualifying figure of a seated woman, is the Egyptian hieroglyph for mother, *mut*—pronounced as in the German *mutter*.)

Many other associations between bird and mother are to be found in ancient cultures. The totems of Mother goddesses such as Ishtar, Aphrodite, and Diana (guardian of childbirth) were often in the form of birds, usually doves. According to one authority, the dove "was in essence always the Great Mother or Aphrodite."[2]

An interesting type of artifact suggesting an association of the breast-mother with another type of bird is composed of two spherical vases connected like Siamese twins so that the fluids in them could mix (fig. 29). Unearthed in the the course of an archeological excavation near the southern coast of Greece,[3] it is one of a number of similar types of vases found in this area and on the shores of Crete. This one, dated at about 1600 BC, was found in the burial site of a young lady and, like others of the period, is thought to have had a ritual function. Each vase shows, on its front, back, and outer side, what appear to be ibises in the act of landing. While the wings and legs are painted in black, the bodies, represented by black circles, are filled in with coral or pinkish colored ochre.

Once again, it is difficult to avoid seeing the obvious—that the two spherical vases, with their coral-pink "nipples," are stylized breast representations. (The style of the period, incidentally, as shown in the gaily painted faience figures unearthed at the Minoan palace at Knossos, left as little to the imagination as the double vase in figure 29.)

An artifact, finally, that leads to the the bird-breast connection through a route similar to that of the "concretion" shown in fig. 14, Chapter 1, is a three inch long sandstone figurine (fig. 30) found in a small Iranian village. Dated at about 1000 AD, it seems to have been worn smooth—presumably by the thumb—on the upper curve of the neck, once more suggesting a rubbing stone and, possibly, a ritualistic oral pacifier.

Like many other animals (the frog, for example), the bird has been encrusted with a variety of symbolic meanings in different contexts. Perhaps the most common is that of the soul, along with several associated meanings, such as the breath of life and the divine spirit. Different sexual meanings for the bird are also common (e.g., the penis), since somewhere in the innermost crucible of human experience all symbols seem mysteriously to merge. Nevertheless, the roundness and softness of the bird (and sounds sometimes reminiscent of nursing, it has been said) make it a natural stand-in for the mother and her breast, from which it is not too difficult to derive associated meanings of soul, divine spirit, and the breath of life. Add to this the bird's mysterious comings and goings, which is much as the infant experiences the mother and her most important appendage, and one can see why the bird has, consciously or unconsciously, been memorialized throughout the ages in folklore and monuments of art and culture as a symbol of the maternal breast. In African folklore the theme of "the bird that made milk" exists in several variants. The bird was also a regular feature in Greco-Roman and early Judaic funerary art, where, although it may not have been consciously recognized as such, it is said to have expressed the hope of immortality, whose prototype has always been the secure nursing situation. No doubt the bird's predictable seasonal reappearances after long absences contributed to the notion of resurrection with which much funerary art is imbued. The pruning hook and the bird on an ancient Phrygian funerary stele (fig. 31) may have suggested, in highly condensed fashion, the inevitability of being cut down by death as well as the hoped for resurrection.

The unconscious equivalence of bird and milk-giving mother has been deduced independently by medieval and renaissance art historians,[4] from

Figure 27
Bird—breast

Figure 28
Bird—breast

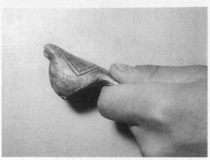

Figure 29
Ibis Jars

Figure 30
Bird Figurine

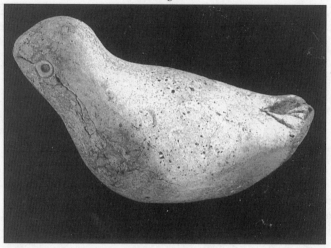

Figure 31
Funerary Stele

Figure 32
"No! No! She's one of mine!"

Figure 33
Composition

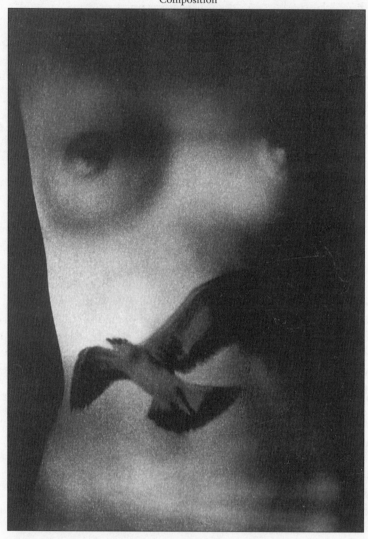

such things (among others) as the number of paintings of the Virgin and Child, which abound from the thirteenth century onwards, in which the Christ Child is depicted either nursing from the breast *or* holding a ball or a bird—usually a goldfinch—in his hand. Art objects or paintings in which the Christ Child is grasping both are rare.

At all events, when adolescent girls think of their breasts as little birds, which they not uncommonly do, they are very likely giving unconscious expression to the same powerful symbolism that has stirred to life in artists from paleolithic times up, which may also be said of the cartoonist of fig. 32 and the creator of the composition shown in fig. 33.

The clinical usefulness of the bird-breast equation was brought home to me some years ago by a curious episode that was related to me by a patient approaching the termination of his analysis. He had awakened that morning with a feeling of absolute certainty that if he went over to New York's nearby Central Park he would, against all odds, see a rare bird called the Worm-Eating Warbler. As a highly knowledgeable bird-watcher he was fully aware that the likelihood of this happening was virtually nil because the bird was rarely seen outside of its breeding grounds in New Jersey, and then only one or two might be reported during its annual spring migration from the tropics. What made it highly unlikely that the patient would see the Worm-Eating Warbler if he prowled the park on this day is that its brief one or two day spring stopover had been reported almost two weeks earlier. Never, to his knowledge, had it been known to make a second visit during this season.

Nevertheless, the patient went to the park, driven by the strange certainty that had taken hold of him. And this feeling, wonder of wonders, proved entirely justified. After only a few minutes of aimless walking he came upon his quarry, unmistakable in its form, color, and markings and flitting about entirely unconcerned with the marvel of its second visitation. With some trepidation (he could hardly depend on the bird to remain in one area for very long), the patient managed to round up several incredulous bird watchers to confirm his find and share in the general wonder of the event. Viewed at close range through a half-dozen pair of field glasses, the bird was unanimously judged to be really the Worm-Eating Warbler.

The patient related these events to me with a profound feeling of awe, accompanied by an almost beatific sense of exhilaration. He was excited not only by the Warbler's unprecedented second visit but also by the uncanny fact of his having felt in advance the certainty that he would witness it.

He seemed to have forgotten, however, that about a year before he had reported a similar occurrence. At that time he had been driving at a leisurely pace along an inland road on Long Island on his return from a day of solitary bird-watching along the shore. Suddenly, while thinking of the fact that he had not seen one Kingfisher during the entire day, the thought came that he was shortly to see one, and this presented itself with absolute conviction. This certainty about what was to be, this preternatural expectancy, had lasted about a minute when a Kingfisher flew right across the patient's advancing car and into the woods alongside.

This event too, at the time, had given the patient a wonderful sense of exhilaration, as if a miracle had occurred, since the Kingfisher, he informed me, while fairly common along the coastal marshes, was rarely seen in the inland wooded regions such as the spot where he had seen it. Equally remarkable to him was the feeling of absolute foreknowledge of the uncommon event about to occur.

Whether or not what the patient had recounted on this earlier occasion was in any way out of the ordinary—it is conceivable that he had first seen the bird out of the corner of his eye or had faintly heard its rattle and had then repressed this precisely in order to give himself the exhilarating feeling of a premonition coming true—the unconscious significance of the 'miracle' was clear. At this time the patient had been at the lowest and most difficult point of his analysis. After a stormy course of treatment he had begun to give up, one after another, a series of self-defeating escapes, including a powerful alcohol and barbiturate addiction, and had finally faced squarely the panic of having to make a living for himself and his family. Just before setting out for his day of bird-watching, in fact, he had finally permitted himself to experience head-on the sad state of debt into which he had fallen and from which he had somehow to extricate himself. And for the first time he realized that he could not go on clinging to a secretly cherished fantasy of a bountiful breast that would somehow present itself in one form or another to magically rescue him from his predicament, a fantasy that had dominated him unconsciously since his severely deprived infancy. All this he had worked through painfully in his analysis, and on the day of the Kingfisher episode, as he was returning from his solitary session of bird-watching, he was acutely aware of his ultimate motherlessness.

This, then, was the setting for the earlier 'miracle,' a miracle that had arisen out of the patient's last desperate attempt to reassert the omnipotence of thought characterizing the early stage of infancy (and the later unconscious in general)—the conjuring up of the mother by merely willing her to appear. For this was plainly the meaning of the sleight-of-mind that had taken place. The unconscious bird-breast equation (it may be assumed that the nominally masculine Kingfisher could be a symbolic mother surrogate simply by virtue of its birdness) enabled the patient to assure himself, even if only, perhaps, through a double-take of normal perception, that all was not yet lost when one could think, "Mother, appear!" and have her then actually present herself. It was this, of course, that had given the patient his unusual sense of exhilaration and had saved him, momentarily at least, from the terrible depression into which the final loss of his unrealistic mother-breast substitutes had threatened to plunge him. It was his version of the spool-on-a-string game of Freud's grandson, of Shaw's waving his playwright's wand to get a resigned Eliza back into the never really outgrown nursery of his alter ego, Professor Higgins.

The episode of the Worm-Eating Warbler occurred, as I have indicated, about a year after the one of the Kingfisher. By this time the patient had come a long way and had reduced his sessions to one a week. He was free of his alcohol and drug addiction, had begun to work again and was well on his way toward being rid of his debts. All the more intriguing, thus, was this seeming repetition of a mechanism whose only purpose could be once more to prove that he could indeed recapture the mother by what unconsciously amounted to the simple act of willing her to appear.

With this in mind, I asked the patient, after reminding him of the Kingfisher episode of the year before, what had happened that made it necessary for him to revert once again to this kind of mechanism for the fantasied control of the mother. What he told me left little doubt as to the correctness of my hunch. To start with, his wife had been out of town for several days and he was alone in the apartment. Then, on the day before the morning of the episode with the Worm-Eating Warbler (on the preceding day, that is), two things happened whose significance could not be missed. First, the part-time maid did not show up to prepare his breakfast and tidy things up. Later she phoned that owing to her daughter's sudden illness she might not be in for several days. Second, when he arrived at his office he found a telegram from his secretary, on whom he had become dependent, stating that she had had to leave suddenly for another city where a family emergency had developed and could not see her way clear to returning at all to the job.

Here, then, we have the absence of one mother figure, the patient's wife, and an abrupt abandonment by two others, the maid and the secretary. The patient suddenly found himself utterly bereft of everyone he had come to depend upon in this role, and this at a time when he was especially vulnerable because of the imminent termination of his treatment, which he unconsciously, of course, experienced as an abandonment by me. Small wonder that he had to fall back on the infantile illusion that he could conjure up the mother by the sheer force of his inner need, the last desperate device of the forlorn child.

A word here about the the depth of the patient's regression in this instance, and the seemingly trivial disappointments that provoked his need for what amounted in his unconscious fantasy to a miracle. It was not, it might be objected, as if the actual loss of a wife or a job were in question. Such an objection has to be flatly and firmly overruled. Any psychiatrist can assure the reader that these trivial "rejections" and "abandonments," these small, inconspicuous accidents of everyday life, are, because of the reverberations they set off in the unconscious, just the stuff that suicides (suicides and homicides, I should say) are made of. What plunges people into major depressive reactions are not necessarily major catastrophic events but more often symbolic shadows, the shards of childhood experiences, that may be imperceptible to consciousness when they are evoked.

So much, in any event, for the power of the bird-breast-mother equation. It enabled me to bring meaning into two seemingly disconnected episodes, which is the essence of what the analyst tries to do. Bypassing the question of *how* the patient was able to achieve his inner feeling of certainty in the Worm-Eating Warbler instance (whether this was another, in this case more cryptic, trick of normal perception or some latent clairvoyant ability need not concern us here), I will note merely that the feeling of absolute foreknowledge that gave the patient his sense of exhilaration in both episodes happens to fit perfectly with the fact that the bird has been associated with prophecy from ancient times, when its entrails were commonly used in the arts of divination. Understanding bird language, moreover, has always figured in folklore as an aid to prophecy, and those endowed with this gift have been thought to be the recipients of some sort of supernatural grace. This, and the fact that a bird flying into the house has widely been supposed to be a forerunner of important news, may be the origin of the saying, "A little birdie told me."

It is not difficult to see why a tie-up between birds and prophecy should exist. What most people have always wanted to know about the future, since the dawn of the capacity for symbolic thought, has undoubtedly been, in one form or another, what every infant wants to know: when will dinner come again. Thus, whether divination or prophecy was ostensibly aimed at when or whether the reindeer (or good fortune) would come, it must always have been experienced unconsciously, as we saw in Chapter 1, in primitive infantile terms. Indeed, our entire experience of time and duration must in some way be conditioned by the primary fact of the periodicity of bodily needs, of which the most urgent, in our most impressionable stage of life, is certainly the need to be fed.

It is not always easy, however, to draw the line between the foretelling of the future and the desire to command and shape it, as both frequently have their root in a more basic need: the need to control the seemingly capricious comings and goings—or, as the infantile unconscious might perceive it, the aimless flittings hither and yon—of the mother and her breast. It is this fantasy of control that is behind the many stories in folklore and literature in which a bird appears at one's command. Indeed, it must unconsciously be part of the fascination of falconry and the breeding and training of carrier pigeons.

One of the most intriguing examples of such a fantasy occurred not in a fairy tale, however, but in the very real life of an acknowledged genius whose accomplishments in the field of electricity and radio rivaled—and in the opinion of a growing number of engineers even surpassed—those of Edison and Marconi. The facts are given in the book *Prodigal Genius: The Life of Nikola Tesla*, by John J. O'Neill, a Pulitzer Prize-winning science editor of the New York *Herald Tribune* and Tesla's close friend for many years.

Tesla, according to O'Neill, was a solitary figure who never had even casual relationships of a sexual or romantic nature with anyone during his eighty-seven year life. Indeed this would have been a problem with his obsessional fear of germs, a paralyzing condition that often has its roots in a difficult neonatal nursing situation and is generally accompanied by a deep ambivalence toward any human affection. (In order not to shake hands with people, Tesla would keep his hands behind his back, but if he were forced by circumstances to do so he would, if possible, immediately retire to wash his hands.)

Tesla's sole relationship of any continuity and depth was with pigeons he kept in his hotel rooms (he was evicted from one hotel after another after it was discovered that he was turning his rooms into dovecotes) and with the flocks of pigeons he fed nightly, with a great deal of secrecy as to what was going on, in New York City's public squares. Near the end of his life he finally confessed to O'Neill, whom he had barred in his earlier years (as he had all others) from accompanying him on his mysterious midnight rounds, the strange facts of his love for a beautiful white female pigeon. The facts were so weird, according to O'Neill, that he might not have credited them had not William L. Laurence, science writer for *The New York Times*, been present as a witness. This pigeon understood him said Tesla, "and I understood her ... I loved her as a man loves a woman, and she loved me." Tesla believed, and confided to O'Neill and Laurence, that he could command his beautiful white pigeon to appear, wherever he was, merely by wishing her to do so. When this pigeon, "the joy of my life," died, Tesla underwent an hallucinatorily vivid mystical experience. "One night as I was lying in my bed in the dark, solving problems, as usual, she flew in through the open window and stood at my desk ... I knew what she wanted to tell me ... she was dying. And then, as I got her message, there came a light from her eyes—powerful beams of light—a powerful, dazzling blinding light, a light more intense than I had ever produced in my laboratory."

The facts of Tesla's life point clinically to a lifelong domination by a "vanishing mother" complex. While he consciously idealized his mother, Tesla managed nevertheless to stay pretty clear of her (he never brought her from her native Croatia to the United States) and throughout his life was given to premonitions of her death, the ultimate disappearance. This kind of ambivalence, typical of hand-washing, so-called obsessional neurotics, marked all Tesla's relationships to mother symbols and mother substitutes. He could not, for instance, stand smooth, round breastlike surfaces, and pearls on a woman were apt to make him physically sick. (One obsessional patient of mine who, according to his mother, had gone into what appeared to be a deathlike depression when he was abruptly taken off the breast at two weeks, couldn't in later life even stand the *word* 'sphere.') At the same time it was his omnipotent fantasy of making mankind's most visible sphere, the sun, do his bidding that gave rise to the idea for which Tesla was perhaps most famous. Walking with a fellow engineering student in Budapest, he watched this oldest of symbols of the all-nourishing source of life as it slowly began to sink over the horizon. He started to quote some lines of Goethe about wishing he could take wing and soar after the disappearing sphere when suddenly he shouted, in a eureka-like exaltation, "But I will reverse it! I will reverse it!" Thus was born the idea of alternating current.

Tesla's attitude toward money was indicative of a deep-lying fantasy of having control of this other virtually universal breast-mother symbol. He gave away millions in gestures of great, if sometimes bizarre, generosity, and was often broke as a result. He was, however, dominated by the comforting belief that fundamentally he was not dependent on fate or other people for his sustenance since he could make money, a trivial and incidental aspect of the tedious mechanics of living, whenever he needed it by coming up with new, patentable and marketable ideas from the inexhaustibly rich reservoir of his own bountiful sphere, his mind.

The most extraordinary facet of this prodigal genius's never-ending game of control of the mother, however, was played out with food itself; but here, unhappily, the negative aspect of his ambivalent attitude toward this most direct of all breast-mother substitutes finally won out. Every evening (in his affluent periods, anyway) Tesla would show up in white tie and tails at either Delmonico's or the Waldorf Astoria, the two most elegant dining places in Manhattan, and be shown to his special table where the following ritual had to be carried out by the head waiter (a highly sought after and costly mother surrogate). Two dozen freshly laundered napkins had to be laid folded beside his plate. "As each item of silverware and each dish was brought to him—and he required that they be sterilized by heat before they left the kitchen—he would pick each one up, interposing a napkin between his hand and the utensil, and use another napkin to clean it." One of his favorite dishes was squab. As a beautiful example of biting the breast that didn't feed him (the other side of his compulsive feeding of pigeons), he would eat only the meat on either side of the breastbone. (A pair of squabs, each topped with a cherry, used to be called "the breasts of Venus" by eighteenth century gourmets.)

Towards the end of his life Tesla, for one reason or another, gave up all his favorite foods, one by one. His method of giving up the things he liked was the ultimate in self-torture. With coffee, for instance, he insisted on having a steaming pot of it always present at his meals, and only when he felt himself no longer tantalized by the aroma—a state which took several years of almost continual agony to achieve—did he feel strong enough to dispense with this spartan practice.

As the wheel of Tesla's inner life came full circle he was reduced to a diet consisting almost exclusively of warm milk. But when his beautiful white pigeon gave forth her last dazzling beams of light—a symbol equated with streams of milk from the breasts from the ancient Egyptians and earlier—Tesla's lifetime of conflict and compensation collapsed altogether. "When that pigeon died," he told O'Neill, "something went out of my life ... [and] I knew that my life's work was finished."

Coming back to bird watching, some years ago the *Saturday Evening Post* ran a cartoon in which a couple of middle-aged men in woodsy garb were training their binoculars, from where they were hidden in a dense forest underbrush, on some members of a nudist colony, the most prominently displayed among whom was an almost too buxom blonde. "I'm afraid this has ruined bird watching for me," says one to the other with a delighted look.

Now, I am not about to suggest that ten million bird-watchers are driven solely by an unconscious identification of bird and breast. It is nevertheless worth emphasizing that somewhere, on some level, in the background of the complex of drives that go into mankind's various fantasies and behaviors relating to birds, the unconscious bird-breast-mother equation is inescapably present. It is as unavoidable as the omnipresent background radiation that fills our earthly envelope. What part this plays in any given instance, and how it might be integrated with other (e.g., scientific, artistic, social) factors going into various ornithological activities, can only be arrived at by detailed investigation of individual cases—hardly called for, obviously, in the case of persons who are enjoying their lives and whatever avian activities they like to pursue. For our purposes, however, we are entitled to entertain useful presumptions about this or that person's inner relationship to birds—to suspect, for example, that Hogarth's use of the outsized bird in his "False Perspective" was, in conformity with what we were able to discern of the latent content of his fantasy, unconsciously dictated by the bird-breast-mother equation. (It is not known whether "bird" as a slang term for woman was in use in Hogarth's time.) In any case, we shall see in the next chapter that Tesla was not the only highly complex person for whom birds seem to have become a dominant passion—at least in part, presumably, on the basis of their still little appreciated symbolic meaning.

Chapter Six
The Lethal Flame

John James Audubon, the controversial nineteenth century naturalist, artist, traveler, memoirist, and adventurer extraordinary, was obsessed with birds. In a well known autobiographical part of his journals titled "Myself" he attempted to explain how this came to be.

> One incident which is as perfect in my memory as if it had occurred this very day, I have thought of thousands of times since, and will now put on paper as one of the curious things which perhaps did lead me in after times to love birds, and to finally study them with pleasure infinite. My mother had several beautiful parrots and some monkeys; one of the latter was a full grown male of a very large species. One morning, while the servants were engaged in arranging the room I was in, "Pretty Polly" asking for her breakfast as usual, *"Du pain au lait pour le perroquet Mignonne,"* the man of the woods probably thought the bird presuming upon his rights in the scale of nature; be this as it may, he certainly showed his supremacy in strength over the denizen of the air, for, walking uprightly and deliberately toward the poor bird, he at once killed it, with unnatural composure. The sensations of my infant heart at this cruel sight were agony to me. I prayed the servant to beat the monkey, but he, who for some reason preferred the monkey to the parrot, refused. I uttered long and piercing cries, my mother rushed into the room, I was tranquilized, the monkey was forever afterward chained, and Mignonne buried with all the pomp of a cherished lost one.

That there was a relationship between this memory and Audubon's lifelong affair with birds is highly probable. But there was certainly much more to the relationship than Audubon was aware of. In the first place, the memory is in some respects rather odd and, like so many things in Audubon's writings, was probably not quite accurate. It shows, in fact, certain of the characteristics of a screen memory, an unconsciously determined slip of the mind whose function, at least in part, is to convey false information. In the second place, Audubon did not only love birds and study them with infinite pleasure; he also engaged in what one biographer described as their "revolting and indiscriminate slaughter." Indeed, another student of Audubon, Roger Tory Peterson, dean of present day bird book authors, wondered how it was that a great national organization dedicated to the preservation of wildlife should be named after a man who "just loved to shoot [and who] made the statement once that it wasn't a very good day unless he had shot at least a hundred birds."

Actually, Audubon didn't love to shoot only birds. He had trigger itch for everything in sight, from buffalo, whose slaughter he took part in and described with almost lustful fascination (he retired for the night after one bloody buffalo massacre "thinking over all God's blessings on this delightful day"), to squirrels, whose killing by exploding the bark under them and sending them whirling into the air (a Kentucky specialty known as the "barking of squirrels") he termed "a delightful sport." And although he wrote that he couldn't bear to see an animal suffering unnecessarily, his notion of necessity seems to have been not too different from that of the notorious Texas Ranger sheriff (after whom John Wayne is supposed to have been modeled in one of his pictures) who is reputed to have said, "I never killed anyone who didn't need killing." Rarely, at any rate, did his often somewhat piously expressed scruples stay his trigger. Some idea of his victimizations can be had from his journals, where he methodically noted how many of each species he had shot (or "killed," a term he straightforwardly used interchangeably with "shot") on a given day—so many Arkansas Flycatchers, so many Sprague's Larks, so many Great Godwits (sixty-five, I believe, in a single barrage). And while he could rhapsodize about how much he admired "every portion of the work of God" after watching "the birds that are always about the place enjoying full peace and security," there was generally little of either of these when he was about. In one place he lists by name thirteen different species—including seventeen parakeets—he and his companions killed within the space of a few hours. And he could write about "the pleasure of seeing a little green-Kingfisher perched close to me for a few minutes" but matter of factly add, after the bird had flitted off after spying him, "I longed for a gun to have stopped him." Perhaps the ultimate in the peculiar dissociation and detachment that so often characterized Audubon's journal entries was achieved when, referring to the anonymous take of "a very dull day," he noted shooting birds of "no consequence."

It should be borne in mind, nevertheless, that for a good part of Audubon's life his primary objective was to paint as many birds as possible, and that he went through prodigious labors and traveled far to compile the material for his universally acclaimed *The Birds of America*. Since handily portable photographic equipment was still a long way off (Audubon lived scarcely a dozen years after the invention of daguerrotypy), there was no way he could achieve accuracy except to sacrifice specimens and mount them in lifelike poses. That he sometimes used as many as a hundred birds for a single drawing has, however, led to severe criticism and condemnation by some of today's ornithologists, even though such extravagance may not have been all that unusual during a period when shooting birds and other fauna was a taken-for-granted part of the lifestyle of every country squire and parson, and few thought anything of the wholesale carnage of egrets for ladies' hats. For many decades after Audubon, as a matter of fact, British railways ran weekend excursions to countryside where birds were so plentiful (ran the ads) that even bad shots could be sure of potting enough to make the day worthwhile; and few eyebrows were raised when Charles Darwin, who spent his youth shooting birds, wrote in *The Voyage of the Beagle*, in reference to the tameness of the birds he encountered in the Galapagos Islands, "All of them approached sufficiently near to be killed with a switch, and sometimes, as I myself tried, with a cap or a hat."

The plain fact is that animal and bird killing for the sheer pleasure and excitement of doing it has long been one of the preferred amusements of man. Some would say, moreover, that killing birds is little different from killing insects or people, which few ever think twice about. Indeed, veteran hunters would probably view the latter day revulsion against blood sports as a pernicious weakening of modern man's moral fiber, all too unhappily apparent on many other fronts in today's insidious deterioration of civilization. There are simply different kinds of people, just as there are different kinds of birds.

All the same, there are dynamics to these differences, and to persons like myself, who are obsessed with people (some of whom, given propitious circumstances, I might feel little compunction about shooting), the fascination of discovering presumptive unconscious factors influencing whether one becomes one kind of person or another is probably just as great as that of finding a rare bird. So although Audubon is hardly the only person who has evidenced what some might deem excessive zeal slaughtering birds ("Three Green-Wings neatly dropped with a double gun," wrote a noted present day conservationist, was one of the things "that make this world a better place than the parsons and the communists say it is"),[1] few have left such an extensive and intimate record of their ambivalent thoughts and behavior in relation to this branch of the evolutionary tree. To this extent, Audubon is a sitting duck (so to speak) for the avid psychoanalytically minded hunter.

Let us begin with Audubon's own account of his birth and infancy, as given in the opening paragraphs of "Myself." This, immediately preceding Audubon's already given account of his curiously persistent childhood memory, has caused endless confusion among his biographers.

The precise period of my birth is yet an enigma to me, and I can only say what I have often heard my father say to me on this subject, which is as follows: It seems that my father had large properties in Santo Domingo, and was in the habit of visiting frequently that portion of our Southern States called, and known by the name of, Louisiana, then owned by the French Government.

During one of these excursions he married a lady of Spanish extraction, whom I have been led to understand was as beautiful as she was wealthy, and otherwise attractive, who bore my father three sons and a daughter,—I being the youngest of the sons and the only one who survived extreme youth. My mother, soon after my birth, accompanied my father to the estate of Aux Cayes, on the island of Santo Domingo, and she was one of the victims during the ever-to-be-lamented period of the negro insurrection of that island.

My father, through the intervention of some faithful servants, escaped from Aux Cayes with a good portion of his plate and money, and with me and these humble friends reached New Orleans in safety. From this place he took me to France where, having married the only mother I have ever known, he left me in her charge and returned to the United States in the employ of the French Government, acting as an officer under Admiral Rochambeau. Shortly afterward, however, he landed in the United States and became attached to the army under La Fayette.

The first of my recollective powers placed me in the central portion of the city of Nantes, on the Loire River, in France, where I still recollect particularly that I was much cherished by my dear stepmother, who had no children of her own, and that I was constantly attended by one or two black servants, who had followed my father from Santo Domingo to New Orleans and afterward to Nantes.

For many years this account, vague and confusing as it is (with Audubon père first *returning* to the United States and shortly afterward *landing* there), was the officially accepted one. Audubon's granddaughter Maria, who arranged and edited the now classic *Audubon and his Journals,* accepted it as substantially correct, although she writes that the death of Audubon's real mother occurred not "in the St. Domingo insurrection of 1793, but in one of the local uprisings of the slaves which were of frequent occurrence in that beautiful island whose history is too dark to dwell upon." As to the date of Audubon's birth, she writes that many allusions to this can be found in her grandfather's journals and letters but that nothing definite can be derived from these sources. "He may have been born anywhere between 1772 and 1783, and in the face of this uncertainty the date usually given, May 5, 1780, may be accepted, although the true one is no doubt earlier."

The facts now known, mainly through the labors of F. H. Herrick, a biologist who spent years tracking down relevant documents, diverge considerably from the account given by Audubon. According to Herrick, Audubon's father, Jean Audubon, was indeed a French naval lieutenant, but little Jean, as John James was called, was born in Santo Domingo, now Haiti, on April 26, 1785. His mother was a Mademoiselle Rabin, a twenty-six year old French Creole whom the lieutenant had met on the ship from France. Mlle. Rabin and Audubon's father were never married as, for one thing, the lieutenant had already been married in France, to a widow some years his senior. Mlle. Rabin did not die in a slave uprising but from illness when Audubon, who was her only known child, was six and one-half months old. The child, known as Jean Jacques Fougère Rabin (Fougère, meaning "fern," was one of the mother's family names), was taken at four and one-half years of age to France, where he was established in his father's wife's home in Nantes. Nothing is known about the intervening years but it is likely that the child was, at least for a time, in the care of another French Creole with whom Lieutenant Audubon had also had a child. This child, Rose Bonnitte, or Muguet, was two years younger than Jean Jacques (or Fougère, as he was sometimes called) and was also taken to France. When Jean Jacques was eight and Muguet six they were formally adopted by Lieutenant Audubon and his wife. Six years later the boy was baptized as "Jean Jacques Fougère Audubon, adoptive son of Jean Audubon, lieutenant of a frigate of the Republic, and of Anne Moinet, his legitimate wife."

The differences between Audubon's account of his earliest years and the facts now known to be true have continued to baffle biographers. To compound the confusion, Audubon's immediate family was given to referring to him as thirteen years older than he was, which some Audubon students believe was done to cover his bastardy. Granddaughter Maria, it appears, took great liberties in the editing of her grandfather's journals to promote such a cover-up. (It is now known, for instance, that a portion in which Audubon confided to his journal in 1843, when he was actually fifty-eight, that he was getting to be an old man, "seventy and over," was actually written by Maria.)

Audubon's own confusion about dates extended, in a most bizarre fashion, to at least one important event in his later life. He wrote in his journal, on August 6, 1826, during a stay in London, that he would like to visit Nantes during a trip he was planning to France, there to see his "venerable stepmother." His stepmother, however, was by this time all too venerable, as she had been dead for five years at the time this was written. This lapse has been set down as an example of Audubon's "whimsicality" by one biographer, and to equally whimsical explanations by others. Curiously, Audubon seemed to know nothing about his stepmother's death even two years later when, according to still another biographer, the news is said to have come to him "as a thunderbolt" in the course of a conversation with someone who had quite innocently referred to it. The lapse was the more remarkable in that Audubon was named as a beneficiary of his stepmother's will.

Let us return now to the persistent memory of Audubon's childhood and see if it can shed any light on what was going on in his peculiarly mixed-up mind. The first thing to note is that this memory itself had become a kind of obsession. Its unrelenting ("thousands of times") repetitiveness, however, indicates that things may not have been entirely what they seemed, and that there may have been something behind what is recounted—a repressed memory, perhaps—that was struggling to get out.

A clue to what this may have been can be seen in Audubon's writing that Mignonne, the parrot, was buried with all the pomp of a "cherished lost one." This phrase, somewhat overblown for what Audubon had a few lines earlier referred to merely as one of several parrots in his mother's (actually his stepmother's) home, and which he had not thereafter singled out and described as the object of any special affection, calls up the image of a past loss, the loss, in fact, of some significant nurturing person. If we recall now the symbolic significance of the bird, we suspect that the real "cherished lost one," for whom the parrot was merely a symbolic stand-in, was Audubon's mother—or some mothering figure—who, like the bird, was supposed to have died by violence.

At this point we have to bring up another version of the imagined violent death of Audubon's mother, although this time it was not the beautiful and wealthy "lady of Spanish extraction" who figured in Audubon's fantasy as his mother but no less a lady than Marie Antoinette, the beautiful and wealthy Queen of France who, with her husband Louis XVI, died under the guillotine. One of the things that has intrigued biographers is that throughout his life Audubon kept throwing out tantalizing hints of having been sworn to secrecy about his real name, of having been of noble birth, of having been born to command, and of not being able to enjoy his rightful status. These intimations somehow fostered the legend, which Audubon did nothing to discourage, that he was really the lost Dauphin, commonly believed to have been spirited out of prison and to a life of obscurity in France or America. Not surprisingly, there were as many claimants to this title as there were, a century or so later, to that of Anastasia, the lost daughter of the Romanovs. Such legends die hard. However, while most biographers dismiss the Dauphin story as just another evidence of Audubon's eccentricity, more than one have attempted to make a case for its validity, placing great stress on the gap in the childhood record and the fact that Audubon's wife seems to have believed implicitly in the story to her dying day.

Alas for the romantically inclined, the story has been thoroughly discredited, not least for the reason that the Dauphin was known to have had a disfigured ear, which Audubon did not. What most biographers could not be expected to know, however, is that such fairy tale fantasies of secret aristocratic or noble birth, known collectively as the family romance, are frequently encountered in children who have lost one or both parents through death or otherwise. These fantasies are considered a grandiose form of denial of the otherwise unendurable hurts to the child's sense of inner worth that typically follow such losses, and they thus aid in the coping process. We recall Descartes' insistence that he was not begot by his parents but, by presumption, by God (than whom you can't get any more noble or aristocratic). In Audubon's case the choice of Marie Antoinette as the mother substitute was singularly apropos since she too, like the mother in the version put forth officially by Audubon, had suffered a violent death in an "uprising." (There is some evidence that Audubon had witnessed a guillotine execution in Nantes shortly after he was brought there.) The anagrammatic connection between *Dau*phin and *Au*dubon could also have played a part, just as in dreams, where such transformations and reversals typically signify death and resurrection. Thus this fantasy could, in effect, have been another screen memory of sorts, a Track Two, as it were.

Coming back to Track One, while it is entirely possible that the incident of the monkey and the parrot described by Audubon could have been based—at least in part—on a true occurrence, it is more likely that it was a crazy-quilt pastiche fashioned out of bits and pieces of reality and fantasy. It could also have included the kind of unconsciously determined word association—"upright," for example, conceivably incorporating an allusion to "uprising"—that goes into creative constructions such as dreams. The real question is why this symbolic melange, whatever its origins, had to play itself out thousands of times, like a broken record.

But in a sense this is exactly what it was. Studies of similar broken records, such as are seen in the traumatic neuroses, show that even when these memories represent a more or less exact image of something that actually took place—say a fatal automobile accident, or the death of a buddy in a shell burst or mine explosion in war, there is invariably something missing from the picture. The missing element is usually a thought or a feeling that occurred at the time of or immediately after the traumatic experience but was suppressed because it conflicted with a more acceptable thought or feeling, such as the horror or grief that might have been appropriate under the circumstances. The unacceptable thought might have been something like, "I'm damned glad that it wasn't I," or, "The sonofabitch got what he deserved." This is apt to appear in consciousness as "It should have been me," accompanied by a sense of guilt because it wasn't. In this way a large and unendurable sense of guilt is replaced by a small and tolerable one.

Which brings us to the denouement of Audubon's mnemonic charade. And here again it is an unusual word usage that is the telltale clue, since it points as clearly as one could wish to the missing element in the memory that kept knocking so insistently at Audubon's consciousness. This is Audubon's description of the monkey as a "man of the woods." Such a designation is surely somewhat forced, if not in fact inappropriate, since the monkey in question—simply a household pet—was in no meaningful sense a man of the woods. Audubon, however, was. At the time "Myself" was written (it is thought around 1835, for Audubon's two sons), he was known internationally as "The American woodsman" and indeed, on occasion, as the "man of the woods." One of his little known French names, moreover, was La Forêt, with whose English equivalent, Laforest, he frequently signed his letters to his wife.

Thus, to whatever degree the recollection of the parrot's demise may have corresponded to some actual occurrence, there are grounds for presuming that in Audubon's unconscious the monkey came to represent

Audubon himself. In fact, it could even have been little Jean Jacques (walking "uprightly" as a beginning toddler, perhaps) who had done the bird in, since children are characteristically given to projecting the culpability for their misdeeds onto their pets. The monkey may just have been the handiest target around for such a displacement. In either case, the hidden unconscious meaning of the memory—its latent content, as it were—would have been the same. For it is highly likely that were it not for the mother (and the breast) that the parrot came to represent in Audubon's unconscious, and for the symbolic equivalence of the two men of the woods, the memory would not have occurred in the form it did, much less as insistently and as persistently as it did.

The memory, thus, can be regarded as a kind of unconscious confession struggling to get out from behind a mixture of cover stories. Significantly, Audubon named his pet sparrow hawk (which he immortalized in his *Birds of America*) Nero. The historical Nero is most often remembered for having fiddled while Rome burned; but, for what it is worth, he also murdered his mother.

We can only speculate as to why Audubon's symbolic matricide—for this is what all the foregoing adds up to—became the dominating unconscious fantasy in his life, along with the need for restitution and atonement that became his life's work. We must presume that a deeply repressed fund of unconscious bitterness and rage against mother figures was built up during the child's earliest months and years. A Doctor Sanson's itemized statement, which is reproduced in Herrick's book, shows that Mlle. Rabin was treated for several weeks prior to her delivery for erysipelas, a highly contagious—and in those days frequently fatal—streptococcal skin infection, and for a breast abscess afterward. Neither condition, obviously, would have made for a happy nursing experience for the child. Indeed, it is quite likely that Jean Jacques had to be put to the bosom of someone other than his mother, at least for a part of the period before her death (the actual cause of which is unknown). The child, in fact, may have been given into the care of several mothering figures between his birth and the time he was taken several years later to his stepmother's home in France. By the same token, he would then have lost a succession of nurturing figures during this hiatus in the record. One of these—possibly the last—may have been Catherine Bouchard, the mother of Muguet, Jean Jacques' half-sister (and only known sibling). Mlle. Bouchard, however, did not accompany the children to France. Nor does it appear that she had any contact with the boy afterward, even though she made the trip to France sometime later. The child Audubon, thus, could have been in a state of almost continual stress and deprivation from his earliest days, one world after another coming to a tragic and desolate end. And even though the step-mother adored and indulged the handsome child who came to her by proxy, her love and support may not have been sufficient to offset and redirect the destructive energies that, in sublimated form, were to become a way of life.

Still, the other side of the picture was just as much in evidence, as is the way with ambivalent feelings and relationships. Birds—even stuffed ones—were Audubon's greatest solace in the periods of profound depression to which he was subject. "Often, after a violent rainstorm, far from my dear home, hungry, wearied, drenched, and lonely," he wrote, "I have blessed the Being who formed the Wood Thrush which has consoled me and cheered my depressed mind ... No sooner are its sweet notes heard than the heavens gradually clear and the great orb of day at length bursts upon the beholder." But just as we are savoring these words we come upon lines such as those Audubon wrote to his family from aboard a river boat: "It is a great pity for us not to be able to go on shore with our guns as we hear the new Meadow Larks singing there."

Such examples spell out as well as anything could the most signifi-cant dimensions of Audubon's complex emotional life. Hemmed in and hobbled by a fateful ambivalence, he was capable of the most casual and sadistic indifference to the very objects that could evoke his most lyrical outpourings of love.

It is difficult to tell from Audubon's many descriptions—often shame-lessly anthropomorphized—of maternal care in the nest (a brooding mother "dreaming of the future;" a mother bird disgorging food into a flock of open mouths after which "the very happy little ones bill with her and caress her about the breast"), whether these are echoes of a fantasied Eden that never was or of a paradise lost. Either way, the unconscious content of such fantasies cannot have been too far from what the infant must have experienced as "the great [if completely unreliable] orb."

Audubon's need to possess and literally (if only symbolically) pin down the capricious breast so that it could never again desert him can best be seen in the method he devised for mounting his specimens. He did this with wires in such a way as to give them a lifelike appearance (a real inno-vation); and it was from specimens thus immobilized and transfixed that he painted and gave to the world an enduring treasure. It is difficult to regard this as anything but a true labor of love even though, paradoxical as it may seem, each painting may also have brought about the death of sometimes scores of birds. The essential thing to see about this love-hate cycle—the pursuit and recapture, the killing, the mounting and the final enshrinement of the symbolic breast in a magnificent work of art—is that it represented a tangled skein of unconscious needs, not the least of which was to effect restitution and atonement for what was unconsciously felt to be a matricide. The memory that Audubon never succeeded in banishing, the murder of the cherished Mignonne by the enraged "man of the woods," was but the dim legend of this symbolic deed of long before.

A significant aspect of Audubon's unconscious ambivalence—and it was undoubtedly deeply unconscious—toward anything or anybody bearing the fateful taint of the early mother can be seen in his treatment of the important women in his life. On one hand he could manifest an extreme reaction to the death of a woman friend of some years standing. According to his own journal account, he was beside himself with grief. "What a void in the world for me," he wrote his wife Lucy. "Many tears fell from my eyes—How can I bear the loss? . . .I wished I [could] have been as quiet as my venerable friend, as she lay for the last time in her room." On the other hand he managed to stay away from Lucy, whom he plainly doted upon, for years at a time while hunting birds over a good part of North America. (Every bird was a rival, Lucy complained.) That Audubon's peregrinations for the most part left his wife scrounging for subsistence for herself and her two sons led one biographer to characterize his behavior as "cavalier and irresponsible." Irresponsibility, however, is not an irreducible character trait. Episodic or chronic, it is always directed against specific persons; and however veiled or rationalized, it is always a manifestation of aggression. Audubon was driven by an inner need for revenge upon all mothers who had abandoned him. His beloved Lucy just happened to be the woman in that tradition who, by very virtue of the love she inspired, could not at the same time escape her role as a potential abandoner. Thus she was fated to play the role of Penelope to his ever wandering Ulysses.

A similar dynamic undoubtedly underlay Audubon's strange denial—for that is plainly what it was—of his beloved stepmother's demise. In Audubon's fantasy this venerable lady never stirred; she just remained sitting where she was when he had last seen her, as fixed as the long dead but secretly exhumed mother in Alfred Hitchcock's "Psycho." If she was not exactly at his beck and call, she nevertheless had no option but to wait until he got around to coming to *her*. It was unthinkable that such an immovable object could just disappear. In Audubon's unconscious fantasy she was just there, like Everest, eternal and unchanging. It took strong evidence to the contrary to change that image.

In his final years Audubon, stricken by hopeless senility, regressed to the ill-nurtured childhood that relentlessly stalked him throughout all the years he himself was stalking, in birds, the mother he never possessed. His friend and long-time collaborator, Reverend John Bachman, wrote to Maria (in a letter now in the Charleston Museum): "The old Gentleman has just gone to bed after having eaten his eleventh meal ...Imagine to yourself a crabbed restless uncontrollable child—worrying and bothering every one & you have not seen a tythe of a description of this poor old man. He thinks of nothing but eating—scarcely sits down two minutes at a time, hides hens' eggs—rings the bell every five minutes calling the people to dinner & putting the old Lady into all manner of troubles ..."

From childhood up Audubon never ceased putting others to all manner of trouble. There is every likelihood, however, that but for such active self-interest and aggressiveness, bred from a fantasy life in which death in one guise or another was an ever present handmaiden, the motherless and repeatedly abandoned child would not have survived.

One of Audubon's nightmares, however, the underside and inevitable accompaniment of his obsession with eating (and birds), I have not yet dealt with. Since this happens also to be one of the the most universal, persistent, and profoundly disturbing—if not potentially explosive—nightmares of man, woman, and society, I shall devote a good portion of the remainder of this book to its origins and some of its many protean manifestations.

Chapter Seven
Ghosts of Infancy

In the fifth volume of his *Ornithological Biography,* Audubon vividly described the horrors he endured in his pursuit of birds. He wrote of experiencing hallucinations in the depth of a forest—"Snakes, loathsome and venomous, entwined my limbs, while vultures, lean and ravenous, looked on with impatience"—and of dreaming, on a sandbar in the Florida keys, "that a huge shark had me in its jaws and was dragging me into the deep."

While it may be that most animals, since the time when the world's population consisted mostly of protozoa, have ended up being eaten by other animals, only a negligible percentage of humans have met their end in this way. Nevertheless, the fear of being eaten, as typified in Audubon's fantasies, is so deeply ingrained in the human psyche that the fact that it is there at all—that indeed there is no culture in whose myths, legends, folk tales, children's stories, and even religious rituals the theme of being devoured by toothy monsters of one sort or another has not been prominent—is, at the very least, somewhat odd. The theme is well represented in the history of Christian thought, from the exegetical writings of the early Church fathers, where Hell was conceived of as a monster that swallowed the wicked, through the middle ages, where the representation of the damned being devoured in whole or in part on judgement day was a regular part of church decor in Europe. A detail of a wooden choir stall showing souls in the jaws of hell is shown in fig. 34. Fig. 35 is from a medieval French cathedral. The most up-to-the-minute metaphor for Judgement Day is shown in fig. 36.

The earliest context in which the irrational fear of being eaten occurred seems to have been in connection with the returning spirits of the dead, which has been reported in all preliterate peoples by travelers, explorers, missionaries, and anthropologists over the past century or two and is presumed to go back to prehistoric times. The supposed reason the dead—or at least their returning spirits—were feared is that they were invariably conceived of as malicious and as often as not given to devouring whomever of the the living they could catch. (Fig. 37 shows a detail of The Scroll of the Hungry Ghosts [Japan, ca. 1200].) With the domestication of plants and animals, however, the spirits of the dead became themselves somewhat domesticated, as they began to channel their malevolent propensities into such comparatively tame pursuits as blighting crops and drying up the udders of milk-giving animals. It was undoubtedly fear of their oral malevolence, in any event, that was responsible for the universal practice of trying to placate them with food offerings. In many cultures it used to be that nobody could partake of a crop until its first fruits were offered to the spirits of the dead.

The most compulsive form of oral propitiation of the dead was seen in classical antiquity, when the living often would hardly wait for a body to become cold before attempting to force feed it. In fact, tube feeding of mouldering corpses was so prevalent in ancient Rome that legislation had to be enacted to stop it. Today the forced feeding of corpses is no longer in fashion but the custom of bringing victuals to the home of the newly deceased is a remnant of the early practice, as is the widespread sin-eater ritual, where a person representing the spirit of the deceased is given a morsel of food to go away and take his evil machinations with him. In our own culture a residue of these propitiatory practices is the Halloween festival, which traditionally takes place on All Souls Eve. Few seem to be aware, however, that the fearsomely got up tykes who parade from door to door on this occasion are supposed to be the dead returning, and that the small offerings of sweets or other edibles that are handed out were originally meant to placate the returnees and divert them from harming—and possibly devouring—the living.

Like the fear of being eaten, the fear of the dead was largely taken for granted by anthropologists, or, circularly, put down to the fact that the dead were, after all, bent on doing harm to the living. One of the few persons who ever asked how it was that the dead came to be envisaged this way to begin with was Sigmund Freud. He addressed this question in 1912 in his controversial study *Totem and Taboo,* and the answer he came up with was, as far as it went, a shaft of sunlight in a subject shrouded in obscurity and confusion. He conjectured that fear of the dead represented the displacement and projection of hostile feelings, notably death wishes, toward those who had died, and he likened this to similar processes in certain types of neurotics. The reason these wishes had to be transformed and displaced, according to Freud, was that in both the primitive mind and in neurotics deeply unconscious wishes were mistaken for deeds in actuality, resulting in an intolerable sense of guilt; and the reason the wish was so overvalued was because it was a remnant of the so-called omnipotence of thought which characterized the earliest stages of man's psychosexual development, the so-called narcissistic stage of infancy. At this stage, Freud held, the child does not clearly distinguish between itself and its needs and what transpires in the external world (which, in infancy, is largely constituted by the mother or other primary caregiver).

There is little doubt that Freud was substantially correct in these conjectures, even though he was far off base in other parts of his brilliant but uneven study. What Freud didn't ask was why the dead should want to *devour* the living and, significantly, blight their crops and dry up the udders of their animals. Granted that if the projection of the hostile thoughts of the living onto the dead were to fulfill its psychological purpose, the dead had to be conceived of as capable of coming back—at least in spirit—in order to return the favor. They couldn't just stay dead—good and dead, that is—without, obviously, short circuiting the process of projection, which was to make it appear that if there were evil wishes around, they were coming from somewhere other than oneself. But there are all kinds of harm the dead could do the living short of devouring them (or threatening to) or taking the food out of their mouths. Why could they not as well be scripted just to cause accidents, illness, death, or all manner of other misfortunes? This, as a matter of fact, would fit well with the way preliterate-primitives, up to recent times according to numerous accounts, envisaged how things actually did happen in everyday life, where there is no such thing as bad luck, only someone's ill will. If someone came to harm, the question always was not how and why did such a thing happen to him in terms of an impersonal causality but solely who, motivated by envy, jealousy, or revenge, *wanted* this to happen and thus *made* it happen.

The answer to why the dead were conceived of as wanting to devour the living—and why in fact the idea of being eaten is so deeply imbedded in the human psyche—lies in an inescapable aspect of the infant's dependence on the mother, namely, its intense reactions to frustration and deprivation during the nursing period. It is here that a predisposition to exaggerated anger and rage at various trigger points, added to whatever genetic factors may play a part, is laid down and incorporated into the developing personality. It is not unreasonable to suppose, therefore, that the death wishes and the guilt early man felt toward the recently deceased were an unconscious repetition of the prototypal affects experienced when mother and the breast disappeared, as they were sometimes unpredictably apt to do during the early nursing period. Because the budding self was not clearly distinguishable from the disappearing object during this period, a confusion as to who was who and what was what was the order of the day, a state of affairs that could play no small part in the development of the tendency toward displacement and projection of thoughts and affects. It goes without saying that these conjectures are also applicable, in hardly lesser degree, to today's populations, even though the omnipotence of thought, unlike the case with early man, where it was the reigning paradigm, has largely gone underground.

At the time he wrote *Totem and Taboo* Freud was mainly preoccupied with his cherished Oedipus complex, and neither he nor his disciples at this time paid much attention to earlier stages of development. Today it is known, from direct observation and experimental studies, that even as early as six or seven months—and maybe even earlier—infants tend to react with anger if something they are given to suck on is taken out of their mouths. Within a few months, especially during teething, this anger can develop into the paroxysms of crying and screaming that look very much like rage to baffled and distraught parents (and to not a few infant investigators). There is, true enough, no way actually to get inside an infant's head during these outbursts and there is consequently no way of knowing for certain that what is being experienced is anything that can be truly be called rage. Nor can we be sure that these outbursts, whatever they represent, are being experienced in relation to—or are being directed toward—the mother and the disappearing soft mass with a nub sticking out of it that is so hard to differentiate from her. It could be that the unhappy infant is just experiencing diffuse depersonalized distress, much as one might feel pain, nausea, dizziness, or any of a number of unpleasant but undirected sensations that flesh is heir to. Whatever the case, psychoanalysts have come to favor the directed rage hypothesis, which they frequently put in terms of the infant being consumed with fantasies of biting, tearing, and devouring the not-always-there-when-wanted mother and her equally uncompliant breast. (Fig. 38 [center], a detail of a medieval pulpit, minces no images on this issue.) The important point, according to classical psychoanalytic theory, is that these fantasies are projected onto the mother and the breast and then return in the form of these inseparable objects—or their symbolic equivalents—threatening to bite, tear, and devour the child (or being destructive in any number of ways—exploding

Figure 34
Choir Stall: Jaws of Hell

Figure 35
Medieval Cathedral

Figure 36
Jaws of Hell

Figure 37
Scroll of the Hungry Ghosts

Figure 38
Medieval Pulpit

Figure 39
*"Don't worry. Fantasies about devouring the doctor
are perfectly normal."*

Figure 40
Nightmare

Figure 41
*"That'll be all for now, Miss Dunn. I have to get ready
for my appointment with my psychiatrist."*

Figure 42
Australian cave painting

Figure 43
"It's called 'Woman.' He finished it just before his divorce in '73."

Figure 44
Kali

Figures 45–46
Steig, *Tropical Fruit*

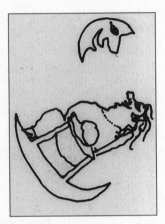

inside the child, for example, or giving poisoned milk). Such a picture is, of course, a metaphorical caricature, more a set of useful symbols than anything else. It does, however, enable analysts to tie together their common experience with an increasingly seen type of patient, whose problems can be best categorized as preverbal, pre-oedipal, oral, and narcissistic, with a wide array of phenomena from other realms. Thus, Audubon's terrifying dreams (and metaphors—his likening London to "the mouth of an immense monster, guarded by millions of sharp edged teeth"),[1] can be put under the same conceptual umbrella as the cannibalistic themes in Little Red Riding Hood, Hansel and Gretl, The Three Little Pigs, and innumerable other stories and myths, as well as a whole contingent of man-eating and otherwise ferocious female demons (one of whom, in Tartar legend, would tickle its victims to death with its oversized nipples). These and a host of other outcroppings and projections from what is sometimes termed the oral-sadistic stage of development—are all, in a sense, modern day ghosts of the hungry ghosts of antiquity.

A large part of the evidence in support of the metaphor of the oral sadistic nursling, however, derives not just from the past history and the symptoms and behavior that bring people to treatment, or patients' accounts, while in treatment, of their everyday problems, or their dreams and fantasies, but their thoughts, feelings, and behavior toward the analyst during the treatment. Contrary to a widely held misconception, the analyst does not always bask in the adulation of adoring patients but is just as often the target of bitter recriminations and attacks on his sincerity, integrity, care, and good will—very much, in fact, along the lines of what a frustrated and deprived nursling might verbalize if it could talk. One patient, who as a child used to fantasy her mother being swallowed by her pet constrictor snake (perhaps along the lines shown in fig. 39) spent several years at this with scarcely a letup. Such rage (the patient's own term, in this case) is, in one degree or another, frequently encountered in what is called the transference neurosis, where the conditions of patients' very earliest years and months are recreated in their relationships to their analysts. Thus while psychoanalytic scenarios about what infants are apt to experience during the nursing period and afterward may well be a kind of mythology, they are far from delusory. What analysts observe on their couches—and what they observe and experience in themselves as they react to the patients' blandishments or assaults (the so-called countertransference situation)—are in a very real sense laboratory data, data that, however deficient in terms of the rigorous canons of the hard sciences, have a degree of validity and relevance that no other method can begin to provide.

For the most part, however, fear of and rage against the breast as such are rarely observed in children or adults. In children these are more apt to surface as fears of disguised or symbolic representations of the breast, such as balloons on the point of bursting, or as terrifying dreams of exploding light bulbs or other spherical objects (recall the exploding gun of the man in the hemispherical arch in Hogarth's pictorial extravaganza of Chapter 4), or of wild animals. (Fig. 40 shows an adolescent patient's sketch of one coming at her in a nightmare.) And although dreams and fantasies in adult patients, both men and women, of biting, devouring, and even ripping the breasts off women—occasionally played out in actuality by severely disturbed Jack-the-Ripper psychopaths and now and again by rapists—are not unknown, as are men (and women) who are given to a hurtful excess of violent biting and scratching during love play, more likely to be encountered clinically are somatic or behavioral equivalents of, or defenses against, such rage, such as chronic teeth grinding (Shaw's Professor Higgins, who was given to this habit, much to the annoyance of his mother, has an army of counterparts in real life in this regard) or specific avoidances, such as of food (self-starved or anorectic persons), milk (quite common), and a host of other breast-mother substitutes. Women themselves may become objects to be avoided (and here again there is an army of counterparts to the misogynous Professor Higgins—Descartes, certainly, for one).

One of the most common avoidances in men, contrary to popular presumption, are women's breasts themselves. A surprising number of men—and sometimes women—simply fail to take official cognizance of these appendages, manage never even to *see* them, any more than the breast-blind artist in fig. 41. Some persons who suffer this perceptual block transfer their love-hate of the breast to the buttocks and achieve orgasm only by whipping these mammary stand-ins or (recalling Desmond Morris' Naked Ape hypothesis about the origin of the breasts as erotic stimuli in the first place) maybe sit-ins. Some years ago one of my patients clued me into a nation-wide underground—a veritable subculture—of buttock beaters and beatees whose participants could be contacted, through private lists, for discreet no-questions-asked rendezvous. Today a number of cosmopolitan dailies and even highbrow periodicals carry notices in the personal columns in which these erotic preferences are either subtly or explicitly conveyed.

With this degree of early rage against and fear of the mother and the breast lying dormant in a considerable part of the population (in females it is normally tempered—though by no means eliminated—by identification with the mother), it is not surprising that the unconscious image of woman has a dark demonic side. In this respect an Australian early aboriginal cave painting of a voracious female demon, shown in fig. 42, is strikingly contemporaneous with the cartoon shown in fig. 43. The archetypal female is seen in her starkest form in the four-armed Hindu mother goddess Kali, at once the creator and sustainer of life and at the same time the cannibalistic devourer of her own children. The predominant object of worship in India, with innumerable forms (I have yet so see one graphic representation that incorporates all her attributes), Kali is frequently shown holding a bowl full of food and a golden ladle (and sometimes dispensing milk from her breast) but at the same time girdled by human skulls and, with one of her free arms, brandishing a wicked looking scimitar. She is also sometimes represented as a hideous hag devouring the entrails of her victims and sucking up their blood with a long animal-like tongue such as is shown in fig. 44.

A considerably attenuated version of this deep lying archetype can be seen in the William Steig drawing shown in fig. 45. Here the underlying terror is defused by the artist's witty caricature of the split maternal image, but there can be no mistake about the cannibalistic lineage ("What big teeth you have, grandmother!") of the the thinly disguised ogress starting on her crescent-shaped melon. (As in the case of Hogarth, the dreamlike emphasis on the crescent, seen in several elements of the drawing besides the lunar crescents—the chair runner, the palm tree and pineapple leaves, for instance—is undoubtedly straight out of the artist's all-knowing unconscious.) Short of Kali herself, a more classic depiction of the two sides of the archetypal mother, both longed-for and feared, would be hard to find.

The one thing missing in all this is any clue to how and when this ambivalence to mother figures and women in general began manifesting itself. It certainly must have been present when the ancient Egyptian hieroglyphic language was developed, since the earlier mentioned root hieroglyph for mother, the vulture *mut* (which in itself seems to be making a statement of sorts), also means "terror and confusion" (another example of the antithetical meaning of primal words in the ancient Egyptian language). That this ambivalence began in prehistory is a reasonable presumption; but while there were the unmaternal "venuses" mentioned in Chapter 1 (fig. 9) during this period, and a couple of uninformative female figures engraved on European cave walls (in one case in bas-relief holding a crescent-shaped animal horn), nothing comparable to the threatening Australian female demon shown in fig. 42 has ever turned up.

An answer to this conspicuous lack is not in sight, given the almost total darkness of this period of history. Except, again, for the possibly negative significance of a few excessively slender figurines, what happened to what one would imagine to be an inescapable other side of the reigning "Great Mother" picture remains completely obscure. Possibly, with magic the order of the day, early humans may have been afraid to concretize their fears—or their rage—by doing anything so risky as putting a lasting representation of this side of the mother on their cave walls.

We shall return to this question in Chapter 9. Let us turn in the meanwhile to several further individual examples of oral ambivalence in action. Beneath the surface of the creative works dealt with we will be able to discern some of the same primal longings and fears, and the same mechanisms for coping with these in fantasy, as were encountered earlier—but in different clothes and with different stage props.

Chapter Eight
Confessional
A Trio of Misogynists

G.B.S.

George Bernard Shaw (G.B.S. to his wide public) vacillated all through his many years between Christian mildness (meekness would have been too much) and pre-Christian thunder and lightning—at least with his prodigiously productive pen. He never went so far in real life as to turn the other cheek, or, despite his carefully cultivated satanic look, assault someone (as did William James on one occasion, just to see what would come of the situation); but in his plays and other writings he did ruminate constantly over the moral dilemma these two positions posed. In his later years, when he found much to admire in the methods, if not always the ideologies, of Hitler, Mussolini, and Stalin, this dilemma ceased to be much of a problem: violence won hands down.

"If a man is a deep writer," wrote Shaw in his apology for not being completely candid in his autobiographical *Sixteen Self Sketches,* "all his works are confessions." And so indeed they are (as I have had occasion to observe in earlier chapters). But it is questionable that Shaw realized what he was letting himself in for when, a few paragraphs further on, he invited psychoanalysts to make what they could of whatever clues had escaped him in these. No analyst worth his couch would pass such an invitation up, or fail to discern in Shaw's works the underlying basis of his often violently expressed destructiveness and enormous ambivalence to women.

Not that Shaw couldn't paint a fetching picture of a thoroughly motherly woman. He did just this in *Candida,* whose protagonist, outside of being a mite too self-conscious about her virtue ("Ask me what it costs to be James' mother and three sisters and wife and mother to his children all in one"), is everything that Shaw's mother wasn't. Most of his portraits, however, are of the other mother.

Consider a scene between a character in Shaw's first novel, *Immaturity* (now deservedly unread), and a deadly, if otherwise dull, barracuda of a husband hunter. "She was sitting near the window when he entered the drawing room. The first thing he noticed was that she had on a dress with a row of conical buttons down the front, which she had worn the last time he had embraced her. Remembering that on that occasion his breast had been dotted by small painful contusions, he resolved to content himself with a kiss." The breast comes on, in this row of conical buttons, as a threatening object.

But even a kiss had its perils, as the hero of another early novel learned when he leaned forward to perform this conventional ritual with his heartily detested mother and experienced only an awkward "collision of teeth."

The novel in which this revealing scene occurs, *Cashel Byron's Profession,* provides a glimpse of a side of Shaw that surfaces repeatedly in his later works and pronouncements. Cashel is by profession a pugilist who early learned the rudiments of self-defense by parrying his mother's blows. Shaw, admittedly ashamed of his own physical cowardice, admired and identified with the strong, from pugilists to fascist dictators. He made himself a first-rate prizefight reporter, and his politics, which he not infrequently expressed in pugilistic metaphors, became increasingly alarming to his old Fabian socialist friends who, at one period in his later years, he insisted greet him with a fascist salute. In *Cashel* an important source of Shaw's marked bully-boy streak is glimpsed in passage after passage where, via the dashing hero (who jests that he eats little boys before going to bed to keep his strength up), violent oral fantasies are unleashed. Sample Cashelties: "You'd better keep your mouth clean if you wish to keep your teeth in it," and "What do you have to say for yourself before I knock your face down your throat?"

Such thinly disguised blood lust and the nothing less than saintly self-restraint of the pugilist-turned-Salvation Army worker in Shaw's *Major Barbara* are, of course, the familiar two sides of one coin. The infantile origin of this uneasy ambivalence may be discerned in the one play of Shaw's in which violence, once the underlying fantasy is stripped of its comic safeguards, appears in its most terrifying form. In *Androcles and the Lion,* which Shaw wrote in less than a week immediately before (significantly) starting on *Pygmalion,* the ancient story is burlesqued in an attempt to deny and contain its nightmarish potential, just as the original legend of the Roman slave who was spared by the lion from whose paw he had once extracted a thorn is in itself an attempt to deal magically with the deep unconscious fear of being eaten. In Shaw's play the source of such a nightmare may be discerned in Androcles' shrewish wife, the image incarnate of last chapter's fig. 38 and undoubtedly Shaw's infantile image of his denying and depriving mother. Although this stock figure, who is made the butt of a lurking male chauvinism that is simply the dialectic of *Man and Superman* reduced to its simplest—and lowest—form, is abruptly jettisoned after the prologue there is little doubt that it carries a message in code (as in all cases where an incident or a character in a novel or a play appears gratuitous from the standpoint of the plot).

The reason why the infantile rage behind the play has to be held in check, at any rate, is that, once unleashed, its destructive potential is beyond control. This is seen in the fearsome Ferrovius who, unable finally to endure the taunts of his Roman captors, forgets all about his lately learned Christian meekness and lays about him with the deadly effectiveness of a threshing machine. The oral derivation of this rage may be seen in the form in which it bounces back, the ferocious lion which is kept specially hungry for its debut in the Coliseum. In *Pygmalion* the fear of being eaten is seen only in attenuated form in such sporadic stage bits as Higgins' complaining to Colonel Pickering, his straight man, that he is worn out monitoring Eliza's teeth and tongue, and his attempts to placate Eliza with a constant barrage of chocolates. In *Androcles* the fear is seen in direct form. The lion, however soft it goes on its benefactor, eats other Christians and whoever is unlucky enough to cross its path with the greatest relish. And although this is given a comic treatment, the underlying horror cannot be completely disguised. In the play as a whole the primal infantile nightmare comes through as a melange of fantasies in which oral aggression and the fear of being eaten are inextricably fused with the fear of tearing one's tormentor to pieces.

Undoubtedly, repression of the fearful fantasies behind *Androcles* (Shaw's "Jaws") must have bred, as it so often does, the evangelical vegetarianism that led Shaw tirelessly to excoriate what he termed the cannibalism of the masses. (By the same token, it must have prompted the powerful apologia for the teachings of Christ making up the preface to *Androcles*.) But these latent fantasies must also have had something to do with Shaw's forthright advocacy, in later life, of the painless liquidation of the masses themselves (specifically, the inefficient, the idle, and the deservedly poor, as well as the criminal and corrupt) and his frivolous flirtation—however often mixed with good sense—with the totalitarian dictators and their methods, which he applauded disingenuously as "weeding the garden" and "cleansing the community." (Hitler, he claimed, should have given him the credit for first putting forth the idea of the gas chambers.) The same fantasies, moreover, were almost certainly related in Shaw's particularly mixed-up unconscious to his rationalizing Stalin's deliberately starving millions of peasants to death. (In *An Intelligent Woman's Guide to Socialism and Capitalism,* he cooly argued that a thousand stomachs could not be any emptier than one.)

It is not difficult to discern in these senile rantings the return of the repressed from repression in sublimated form, the rage of the psychological starveling who also gave us *Pygmalion* and a score of other works of unparalleled brilliance. I forget whether it was the actress Ellen Terry or Mrs. Patrick Campbell, the original Liza Doolittle and Shaw's other long-term platonic unamorata, who wrote in exasperation, after one of his non-stop epistolary scoldings, that someone should have said hush to him in his infancy. It might have been even better, perhaps, had someone said, "Hush, my darling, my sweet, my very own, Mommy's right here."

Hitch

Cannibalism might be too strong a term for the masses' disdain of a vegetable diet (after all, mankind grubbed for roots long enough) but it might not be all that inapt in the case of Alfred Hitchcock who, at his 300 pound plus prime, was capable of putting away three steaks, each followed by ice cream, at a single sitting, and whose behavior towards people, particularly women, often verged psychologically on the cannibalistic. That the origin of such Gargantuan oral cravings is held to be in the same kind of early deprivations (with or without the conjunction of a few other contributing influences) as in the case of Shaw's vegetarianism and Nikola Tesla's heroic later-life self-denial never fails to exasperate critics of psychoanalytic theory. But this paradoxical state of affairs—cousin to the linguistic situation mentioned earlier—happens to be less theory than repeatedly encountered clinical fact. No one is quite sure how this curious either/or development comes about, but analogies to it, in addition to the linguistic ones, can be found everywhere in physiological and biological systems, where opposite types of reactions to similar contextual situations—often termed "paradoxical reactions," in fact—are frequently found to occur.

There is little question, in any case, that the fact of Hitchcock's mommy not being right there when he wanted her as an infant dominated his life and work. Indeed, much of what he did (besides overeat), thought, and put into his films can be seen as unconscious attempts magically to reverse or undo that infantile situation and, just as importantly, to punish the woman who was responsible for it. All of this is hinted at in a curious bit that found its way into a television interview with the then acclaimed dean of American suspense films aired at the very zenith of his career. In his characteristic deadpan manner, he remarked that "people like to be scared, to suffer because their mothers said 'boo' to them when they were about six months of age." When asked if his mother had said "boo" to him, his unsettling reply, even more deadpan (if that were possible), was, "I don't know, I wasn't there."

Outside of his phenomenal early rise to success as a film director, Hitchcock's external life was hardly a biographer's dream. At 21 he obtained a job in the British Famous Players-Lasky and soon became an indispensable factotum who could do everything the company needed done, including direct their films. But thereafter it was just one film after another. Hitchcock's florid inner life, however, early gave promise of the direction his career in films would take. Something of this can be glimpsed in a short short story—less than a page (signed "Hitch")—he concocted for an advertising company magazine when he was still in his teens. Its heroine (there was no hero), "a vision of affrighted purity," was seized by a group of drunken men. "No, not that," raced through her mind, "Anything but that!" But the men, interested apparently only in doing away with her and sharing her belongings, took her to the river and threw her to the hungry water rats. Just as she was sinking to her doom, with the odd phrase "The rats shall feast," running repetitively through her mind, the dentist (a dentist *ex machina*, obviously) brought her out of her anesthesia and announced that her tooth was out.

From a lonely and secretive little boy Hitchcock grew into a lonely and secretive man. When he was 16 his father died, leaving him to take care of his mother, who continued to be the doting but demanding center of his life even after his marriage at 27 to his assistant scriptwriter and set designer, Alma Reville (who continued to be an indispensable part of his professional life). Up to the time of his marriage Hitchcock had been made to stand nightly at the foot of his mother's bed to give an account of his day in what he later remembered as the "evening confession." (Something like this was repeated between the suave Nazi, played by Claude Rains, and his tyrannical countess mother in Hitchcock's 1946 *Notorious*.) Afterward, attendance on his mother was continued with as much constancy as circumstances allowed, including having her along on many of his and Alma's holidays, and building a house for her next to their weekend retreat in Surrey.

Whatever Hitchcock's inner life was like, little of it surfaced from under his characteristic phlegmatic facade—except in his films and his practical jokes. The latter—which became almost as famous in film circles as Samuel Goldwyn's malapropisms—were notoriously sadistic, especially towards actresses. Toward these he followed a rule of Victor Sardou, a popular French playwright, *"Torturez la femme."* It was best to "break 'em down at the very start," he told one interviewer.[1] This he did by humiliating them or demeaning them in some way, which he called "taking the mickey out of them." His method of taking the mickey out of Madeleine Carroll, the female lead in *The 39 Steps,* was particularly revealing. A key bit of business in *The 39 Steps,* as was mentioned in Chapter 3, was having the hero and the heroine manacled together while fleeing their pursuers. To show Carroll and her leading man, the actor Robert Donat, how the scenes they were to play while in this predicament were to be shot, Hitchcock clamped a set of handcuffs on them after which, claiming to have misplaced the key, he disappeared for the better part of the day. He later made inquiries among the studio crew about how the pair had managed to tend to their personal needs. No one was amused.

Hitchcock often referred to actors as mere "cattle" who had to be trained to do what they were told. Alma too fell under this rule. On being knighted, near the end of his life, Hitchcock was asked what he thought his wife's reaction would be. "She'd better mind her own business," he replied, "and do as she's told." Ostensibly said in jest, this was no joke to Alma, who remained a slave virtually manacled to Hitchcock up to his death. Her rare absences were, however brief, unendurable to her Master, whose anxiety would mount perceptibly until she reappeared.

It hardly requires a psychiatrist to underscore the depth and pathological nature of Hitchcock's attachment to his mother. Nowhere is this highly "divided" obsession shown better than in his cinematic use of birds which, from his earliest films, he would work into his plots in odd, dreamlike ways—almost certainly with no more idea than Audubon of the bird's profound symbolic significance.

In his 1930 film *Sabotage* birds figured prominently in connection with the themes of terrorist aggression on a rampage, guilt, and retribution. One of the chief characters in the film, whose major incident was loosely derived from Joseph Conrad's *The Secret Agent,* is a Mr. Verloc, the proprietor of a run-down movie theatre in a lower middle class neighborhood. This—one of the many things in the film not in Conrad's book—is a cover for his major occupation as a professional saboteur working for a higher-up who runs a bird shop (also not in the book) as a cover. We are introduced to the latter, ostensibly a quite ordinary shopkeeper but as clearly as the Greek Furies a structuralization of rage, when a woman comes into his shop to return a caged canary she insists will not sing. After she leaves Mr. Verloc comes in and is told that his next job is to plant a bomb which, set to go off that day at 1:45 p.m., will be delivered to him in a bird cage (another gratuitous Hitchcock bit). The cage is duly delivered with a bomb wrapped in a movie film container inside, and a note stating, "Don't forget, birds will sing at 1:45." Mr. Verloc removes the wrapped bomb from the cage and is about to go on his way with it when he discovers that he is under surveillance by Scotland Yard. In desperation, he asks his wife's young brother, whose special interest in birds has already been shown in several episodes, to take the package to its destination across London. (The boy is shown whistling at a couple of caged canaries, at this point.) Although he has plenty of time to make the delivery, the boy, unaware of the object of his mission, dawdles at every turn and is soon leaving little time for unanticipated delays, such as traffic jams and a Lord Mayor's Day parade. (At intervals clock faces are shown with their hands relentlessly advancing.) The fatal final delay occurs when he stops to find out what a circle of people are looking at. Jostling his way through the crowd, he sees a street vendor hawking his wares. Just as the boy turns to leave the vendor singles him out as the person on whom to demonstrate his new improved toothbrush. The protesting victim is dragged back and forced into a chair where the 'Professor' uses him, to the boy's evident discomfort, for a needlessly rough demonstration of how teeth should be properly brushed. When he finally escapes from this oral mayhem being visited upon him, the boy boards a crowded bus, plays with an appealing puppy held by the person on the seat next to him and, promptly at 1:45, is blown to bits, along with everyone else in the bus. When his sister discovers what had happened she faints, just as the movie in the theatre is showing, appropriately enough, "Who killed Cock Robin?" a Disney cartoon.

Coincidentally with the repeated use of birds and bird themes in the picture, its main interstitial stuffing and anxiety buffer is an extraordinary and seemingly idle amount of attention to food, the discussions of menus, and the business of eating. Neither this nor the bird episodes are strictly necessary from the standpoint of logical and economical plot elaboration. Like other gratuitous devices in his films, they were introduced by Hitchcock himself. (Only Peter Benchley's book *Jaws*, not altogether surprisingly at this point, can match Hitchcock as regards the sheer number of gratuitous descriptions of food, menus, and the business of eating.)

The sudden death of the young boy, for which the viewers were totally unprepared in the sense of imagining that it could actually happen, and especially the brutal way in which it was brought about, shocked the British public and critics, as well as audiences in America, where the film was shown as *Woman Alone.* And indeed, outside of Beerbohm's *Zuleika Dobson,* where the same anti-Aristotelean device is used with tongue in cheek (one of a group of university students, for whom the reader has been carefully seduced into positive feelings, trips as he tries to jump out a first floor window "and was, I regret to say, killed"—end of character), nothing of this sort, which defies a basic canon of dramaturgy, had ever before, to my knowledge, been deliberately sprung on readers or viewers (although similar devices have been used once or twice since). Characters are never rudely wrenched away from audiences who are settling into a dramatic presentation with the usual set of culturally learned expectations. But the totally unbuffered snuffing out of the young boy is apparently precisely what Hitchcock intended: perhaps he wanted to make the audience experience as sudden a loss as he had as an abandoned child, especially in his child's fantasy. It was as if, in doing this, he revenged himself upon an uncaring mother. The boy who was blown to bits, moreover, could have been none other, in Hitchcock's violent unconscious fantasy, than the child he himself had been when, in effect, he was destroyed by a dangerous maternal device over which he had no control. (Let us recall the puzzling exploding gun in the arch of the bridge in Hogarth's drawing.)

Hitchcock's seemingly gratuitous use of bird themes occurred in several films after *Sabotage.* In one of these (*The Lady Vanishes*), for example, there is the sudden one-shot materialization of a flock of pigeons from a magician's baggage. (The film hinges on the sudden disappearance of a kindly old mother figure who provides food for two stranded travelers at its beginning; at the end she turns out to be a secret agent.) Birds were never more tellingly used, however, than in Hitchcock's two most controversial shockers, *Psycho* and *The Birds,* made in 1962 and 1963, respectively. In each of these the theme of attachment and abandonment is central to the plot, but it is in *Psycho* that a principal character—and this time an established figure in real life, the actress Janet Leigh—is again dangled before the audience and suddenly destroyed in a particularly brutal manner (she is slashed to death in a shower stall) with the picture scarcely under way. It is as if Hitchcock were once more bent on having the audience experience just what he experienced as a child when his mother abandoned him.

The central twist of the plot is not revealed until the very end of the film, when the psychotic killer's ambivalent attachment to his mother, whom (as mentioned in Chapter 3) he has kept as a rotting skeleton in the attic of his house, is explained to assorted representatives of the law by a psychiatrist conjured up for the occasion as a sort of retrospective *deus ex machina*. In a summary overview of the case, the psychiatrist explains that the son, who runs the old family motel, poisoned his mother and her lover after discovering their relationship but that he could not let go of his mother even though it meant exhuming her not too well preserved body and setting it up in the attic. The ultimate in possessing the mother, however, as the psychiatrist explains, is to *become* her, which the son does by secretly dressing in her clothes, speaking in her voice and finally not even knowing whether he was himself or his mother. That it was in his mother phase that he committed the shocking murder in the shower tells us (if not the psychiatrist in the film) something about the projective nature of his intense rage against the mother. The audience is brought unconsciously to focus on this theme by the angry remarks the son makes about his mother—that he sometimes hates and curses her but can't leave her— during a conversation with the soon-to-be-murdered new guest at his motel (for whom he has just rustled up a snack by way of a last meal). Just as significantly he talks of aloneness in general, of what it means to be alone with just one's mother, and even of how alone his mother felt when his father died. But he also makes oddly gratuitous remarks about his hobby of stuffing birds, specimens of which are in fact plainly in view all over the place during this scene, as are bird pictures on the wall. Although Hitchcock, as already indicated, could have had no conscious inkling of the symbolic significance of birds (which, at the time, was the esoteric knowledge of only a meager handful of persons), he could nevertheless have hardly achieved a better audience preparation for what was about to take place had he introduced subliminal images of breasts.

The shocking murder scene takes place within seconds after the victim (we can't call her the heroine, since she is trying to make off with a bundle of money she has stolen from her firm) is suggestively shown undressing before stepping into the shower. What follows in the shower is thrust at the viewer in a sudden ambiguous flurry of shots in which the murderer's knife is shown slashing downward with a fury that seems almost to slice through the film itself. That the intended target was the victim's breast is plain, despite the deliberately confusing cinematography, as her frantic arm movements are entirely in front of her chest in her initial attempts to defend herself against the downward slashing knife. A quick final shot shows the knife aimed at the abdomen, but this may well have been only to allow the film censors, the critics, and a shocked public to deny the intolerable perception of Janet Leigh's breast being slashed—which, in fact, is the whole point of Hitchcock's contribution to the film. (In the book from which the film was adapted, Robert Bloch's *Psycho,* the victim is decapitated.) That Hitchcock deliberately intended to convey the inner image of the victim's breast or breasts being slashed is indicated by his deft introduction of an unequivocal breast symbol just prior to and also immediately following the slashing, a fleeting but riveting head-on view, as inescapable as a huge exclamation point, of the circular shower head and its central nipple, with nothing else in the film frame except the water gushing from its numerous spouts. If there is any conceivable explanation for these startling but otherwise quite irrelevant shots beyond the director's deliberate attempt to implant in the viewer the subliminal idea of BREAST-BREAST-BREAST!, it is certainly not obvious.

Nor is the reason for the murderer's offering milk to his potential victim immediately preceding the conversation mentioned above in which he angrily expresses his resentment toward his demanding mother. (The murderer carries in a cinematically intrusive white half-gallon milk pitcher on a platter.) This bit of stage business is so obviously contrived in its logical irrelevance as to almost impede the flow of the story. Indeed, it would have been far less needlessly intrusive had the murderer casually said something like, "Would you care for a cup of tea?" or "How about a coke?" (In the book it is coffee.) Only in *The 39 Steps,* made 25 years earlier, was the connection between milk and murder made as explicit. In that film too the hero offers a snack to the unidentified woman who has accompanied him to his flat just before she is mysteriously stabbed in the back—but not before she is suggestively silhouetted with the focus on the curve of her breast. The crowning point is reached when the hero, fearful that he would be suspected of the crime—as well he might be (he is psychologically the murderer), escapes in a white cap and uniform borrowed from a milkman who just happens to be handy. (It is after this that he manages to get himself manacled to the reluctant heroine.)

A final bit of stage business in *Psycho* that Hitchcock introduced in his sure dreamlike way was to have the murderer accidentally knock one of the bird pictures off the wall following his grisly deed. This undoubtedly came straight from the deepest layers of Hitchcock's unconscious since, as has been emphasized, he must have been consciously unaware of the symbolism involved. As it was, its effect was like dropping a period at the end of a sentence, a way of saying, "Well, that's that." Hitchcock's chief unconscious business was over and done with. The rest of the film was merely the conventional spinning out of a cops-and-killer story that could easily have been turned over to someone else, like a surgeon assigning the final stitches to an assistant before peeling off his gloves and leaving the operating room.

But Hitchcock had not yet done with the unconscious nightmare that had been pursuing him since his lonely childhood. What remained was the final act of the complex fantasy drama, the return, in some form, of the biting oral rage that had been projected outward. Thus there was a kind of classical inevitability in Hitchcock turning, immediately following *Psycho,* to a theme whose essential content must have been lying uneasily in the depths of his mind at least since "The Rats Shall Feast" story he had written more than four decades earlier, the theme of being eaten alive. In 1950 he had toyed with the idea of doing something with a story of cannibalism, but he didn't get around to the root idea again until weeks before he got busy with *Psycho,* when he did a teleplay, *Arthur,* in which birds are used not only to convey something sinister in the atmosphere but as actual instruments of a cannibalistic fantasy. The murder method in this piece is actually strangulation (one of Hitchcock's favorite means of mayhem, a preference shared in fantasy by many orally fixated persons and by some in actuality) but the body of the victim, a woman, is then ground up and fed to the chickens. The projective nature of the grisly infantile fantasy underlying this came to the surface in *The Birds,* which Hitchcock adapted two or three years later from a Daphne du Maurier short story with that title. In it an entire community is attacked, with seeming malevolence, by frenzied mobs of birds. In the du Maurier version, however, the theme is treated in a fundamentally mechanical way, as an inexplicable and psychologically meaningless occurrence in the life of a community. There is a sense of disaster but not of doom, or of some mysterious evil on the loose. This might also have been the case with the Hitchcock version but for his special personal touch which, deriving directly from his ever provident unconscious, infuses an otherwise poorly contrived and even silly script with universal unconscious appeal.

What Hitchcock added to du Maurier's bare mechanical plot were several sub-themes having to do with the pain and anger of abandonment which, from the standpoint of conventional plot elaboration, made little sense but, in terms of the symbolic significance of the principal theme— breasts biting back, so to speak—gave the latent content of the film an overall coherence that somehow got through to audiences. (*The Birds* became a smash hit.) Shortly after the start of the film, following a wildly improbable sequence in which the socialite heroine (played by Tippi Hedren, Hitchcock's latest in a long line of Galateas) tracks a handsome stranger to his weekend retreat, there is a scene whose significance at once sets the stage for what is to follow. With almost total irrelevance from a standpoint of logical plot elaboration, the socialite, who up to this point has hardly said two words to the puzzled target of her attentions, angrily blurts out that her mother permanently "ditched" her when she was a child. Immediately following this, as an ominous prelude to what is to come, she is inexplicably attacked by a dive bombing gull (the action takes place on a bay in California) which bloodies her forehead. This sequence—the theme of abandonment followed by a bird attack—is repeated throughout the film. No sooner, at any rate, does her host, the now piqued male lead, return after fetching some band-aids than his widowed mother comes on the scene and begins shooting dirty looks at the intruder, whom she senses might come between her and her son. The unwelcome heroine then has a talk with a woman who, presumably at the instigation of the apparently perennially threatened mother, had been jilted by the son several years earlier but has taken up residence in a bleak, lonely community across the bay in the hope that she might catch sight of her former lover from time to time. Soon whole flocks of crows and gulls begin attacking the community with increasing fury, forcing their way down chimneys, breaking windows and splintering whatever walls and doors they can thrust their savage pile-driving beaks into. Somewhere in the middle of this, with pecked-to-death, eyeless bodies beginning to pile up, the terrified mother makes a vehement speech—again seemingly gratuitously—about how helpless and alone she felt after the death of her husband. Around this time in the film, also, a Greek Chorus of townspeople huddling in the general store accuses the "ditched" socialite newcomer of bringing the mysterious catastrophe upon them. Now it is her turn to become the target of a vicious avian attack, which is shown in frightening detail. We see her flailing away at the birds much as the victim in *Psycho* tried frantically to ward off her attacker's knife. Just as it appears that there is little left for her but to become birdfood she is rescued by the man she has somewhere along the line fallen in love with. The film ends with him leading her, his mother, his daughter and, contrary to all conventional criteria of what ought to make a reasonably good film, an inexplicably involved audience to safety.

Hitchcock, curiously, seemed more closely identified with the birds than with his leading lady. Whether or not he was deliberately trying to follow his "torture the woman" formula during the filming of the vicious bird scenes, there was little doubt in any of the horrified studio crew's mind that he succeeded to a potentially dangerous degree in reality. The birds used in the shooting of the film were specially trained to swoop in and dart towards their human targets without actually harming them. But when for some reason Hitchcock became obsessed with getting an Oscar winning performance out of them in the scene in which the heroine is almost pecked to death, things went frighteningly wrong. He made Hedren and the supposedly letter perfect birds repeat the scene over and over again for several days on end, with Hedren becoming increasingly terrified and exhausted. Finally, the birds began to blow their lines and actually attacked Hedren, with the result that she collapsed on the set and, on doctor's orders, had to remain away from the studio for a week.

The sad business with Hedren came to an end in a way that only the Marquis de Sade, who knew all about inflicting pain (and even killing) out of frustrated longing, might have anticipated. Hitchcock became more and more openly infatuated with the woman he had sadistically exposed to needless danger and, by the time of the shooting of his next picture, *Marnie,* in which she was also starred, there was hardly anyone in the studio who didn't know about it. On and off the set he mooned around like a love-crazed adolescent, pestered the object of his crush with his romantic dreams about her, wrote her mash notes, and became insanely possessive of her.

This all came to a head, according to Donald Spoto in his tirelessly researched *The Dark Side of Genius: The Life of Alfred Hitchcock,* when, in "an ugly moment of crisis," Hitchcock made an open sexual advance to Hedren in her dressing trailer. (This occurred at a time when, by his own admission, he had not had sexual relations with Alma—or, almost certainly, with any one else—for thirty years.) Summarily rebuffed, Hitchcock threatened to ruin his appalled and shaken star by cutting off her income so that she couldn't continue to help her parents, to get her blacklisted in effect from all major work, and to reduce her to the nobody she was when he picked her up. His personal and professional decline, which soon set in, has been traced to these events. *Marnie,* which became an emotional white elephant in which Hitchcock seemed to lose all interest, was a total flop.

Towards the end of his life, as his powers ebbed and senile memories took over, Hitchcock would blubber to what friends remained to him about his parents leaving him alone at night. Apparently nothing in his entire life—the fame, the money, and even the joy of creating films in which his sure translation of dark unconscious depths, to say nothing of his innovative technical mastery of his chosen medium, had few peers—ever made up for that. He died a lonely, emotionally impoverished child, possessed wholly by the inner drama of *Psycho, The Birds,* and, ironically, *The Rats*

Shall Feast, a creation whose outer drama might not even have got him a passing grade in a high school English class.

Charlie

In a remarkable sequence in his film *Modern Times,* Charlie Chaplin uses a theme that is a psychological clone of the one used by Hitchcock in *Sabotage* in which the young boy is dragooned into a street vendor's unnecessarily rough demonstration of a new improved toothbrush. In Hitchcock's version the assault, with the boy forcibly held in restraint, occurs minutes before he is blown to bits by what is symbolically an angry breast (a bomb delivered in a bird cage with the note "The bird will sing at 1:45"). Chaplin's version lacks the symbolic undertones but is far more direct in its reference to what any analyst, if this were to occur in a dream, would unhesitatingly interpret as a derivative of an unpleasant nursing experience. In this version Charlie is singled out from his fellow assembly line workers in a state-of-the-art industrial plant to be the guinea pig in an experiment with an automatic feeding machine whose purpose is to greatly reduce the time required for the workers' lunch periods. After he has been installed and rendered immobile in a sort of dentist's chair straitjacket, the machine commences to deliver to the general region of his mouth, by means of a mechanical arm, a succession of edibles and drinkables—a bowl of soup, corn (on something like a revolving typewriter platen), chunks of meat, a creamy desert. He is supposed to fend and feed as best he can in this situation with his lips and whatever slight movements of his head are still possible. After each course something like a swiveling mechanical blotter is delicately brought to his lips as a mouth wiper. As each part of the cycle is demonstrated to a fascinated circle of supervisors and executives by the proud (but obviously quite mad) inventor, it is apparent that the totally bewildered and utterly miserable guinea pig is having a hard time keeping up with what is demanded of him and his put-upon mouth. But this is nothing compared to the chaos and mayhem that results when the machine goes out of kilter, as it does almost immediately when it dumps a bowl of soup into Charlie's lap and begins blindly to shove into his battered mouth chunks of food, misaligned parts, loose nuts, gooey pies, and whatever else it can scoop up. The look on Charlie's face is one of sheer horror. (At this point the factory boss quits the scene with the pronouncement, "It isn't practical.")[2]

   If any support were needed for the presumption that behind this excruciatingly funny sequence was a painful early experience of maternal deprivation and rejection, the remainder of *Modern Times* abundantly provides it. Charlie hardly takes his place again on the assembly line than he suffers a nervous breakdown and goes berserk. Unable to stop spasmodically jerking a pair of wrenches he used to tighten bolts on the assembly line, he runs around looking for anything that appears tightenable. When he takes after a full-bosomed passerby on whose bodice, directly over the nipple areas, he spots hexagonal buttons that look like a promising pair of nuts for his wrenches, he is hustled off to a mental hospital. Following his release there ensues a series of adventures and misadventures with and fantasies about food and eating. The most revealing of the latter is a daydream whose point is to provide Charlie with just the right balm for his horrible experience with the automatic feeder. In it he and a carefree gamine he has taken up with are in their dream house where succulent fruits practically fall into their hands from trees just outside the open windows. The table, set for two, is laden with delicious food. A cow ambles up to an open doorway and, with never a word said to it, sprays its milk into a pail conveniently at hand. Dismissed by Charlie with a lordly gesture, after it has filled the pail and thus fulfilled its destiny, it ambles contentedly away. A more perfect representation of complete control of the comings and goings of the nursing mother—even better than Professor Higgins ordering Eliza to fetch him a ham and cheese as he settles complacently into the divan with the slippers she has brought him—can hardly be imagined.

Later in the film Charlie deals with the painful experience of the automatic feeding machine (and the prototypal experience behind it) with the mechanism of reversal rather than of denial. Instead of transforming the experience into its nirvana-like opposite, this time he arranges things in fantasy so that now *he* is the active controlling agent while someone else is the passive victim. In the mad confusion surrounding Charlie's breakdown the plant's electric power fails and Charlie's supervisor (played by Chester Conklin, Charlie's walrus mustachioed straight man whose forte was comic understatement) is accidentally entrapped in the frozen gears of a huge machine. Like Chaplin in the feeding machine, he is unable to move any part of himself but his mouth and to a slight degree his head. Charlie comes to the rescue with a reamed out chicken through which he is able to funnel some soup into the hapless victim's mouth.

The choice of a male figure for the victim in this scene is curious in that, given the creative latitude of Chaplin's films (he frequently improvised several variants of a given theme before deciding on the finished version), it must easily have been possible to have conjured up a story line calling for a symbolically more suitable woman in this role—that is, as the person to be punished in some form of a reversal of the feeding machine bit. However, the choice of a male figure for this role may have been influenced by factors deriving from a phase of Charlie's infancy somewhat later than the nursing period but, in its way, just as traumatic. For residues of this we have only to turn to another of Chaplin's films, *City Lights,* which premiered in 1931, five years earlier than *Modern Times.* In this film Charlie saves a hard drinking millionaire from drowning himself in despair. In gratitude the millionaire takes Charlie to his heart, but he is curiously unpredictable. When he is drunk Charlie is his best friend, and he can't do enough him. When he sobers up he can't recall his little friend of the night before and orders him thrown out of his house.

Chaplin early learned the unpredictability and unreliability of human relationships. From his infancy on people seemed to just come and go and, what was worse, to change from being one self one moment to being someone quite different the next. When he was about sixteen months of age his alcoholic father, a fairly successful music hall singer, left London, where Charlie was born in 1889, for a two-month tour in the United States. He returned to find his marriage to Charlie's mother Hannah, also a music hall singer, on the rocks. Within a year Charlie's mother took up with another music hall artist by whom she had a son when Charlie was not yet two-and-one-half. About six months later this man, also alcoholic—and reputedly prone to violence with all his wives (he had three) and lady friends, forcibly snatched Charlie's new half-brother from the distraught Hannah (from whose earlier marriage Charlie already had one half-brother) and took off for good. Not long afterward Charlie's eccentric and alcoholic maternal grandmother, whom Chaplin remembered only as a bright little old lady who always greeted him effusively with baby talk, was certified as insane and sent to the London County Asylum.

The loss of his father, then of his stepfather (or at least his mother's lover) and finally of his grandmother could not but have been painful experiences for the infant Charles. The first two, in fact, quite likely played significant parts in the unconscious choice of a man as the victim helplessly immobilized in the frozen gear episode in *Modern Times.* Such a figure could well have been a compromise between the depriving mother and an abandoning father, since double-duty castings of this kind are common in dreams and literature and indeed are played out constantly in analytic therapy, where the analyst becomes mother or father in turn—or, as sometimes befits the unconscious situation, both together. That Chaplin's mother was also mentally ill off and on during this early period is more than a remote possibility. Chaplin remembered her about this time as subject to acute headaches but as otherwise a devoted mother scrounging (not always successfully) to keep herself and her children out of the workhouse. But he also remembered her during this period as often singing, dancing, and miming to his and his half-brother Sydney's delight. While this may have been innocent enough it is suspiciously like the inappropriate singing and dancing that, along with incoherent and delusional behavior, the medical authorities noted in one of her later asylum stays. The first record of what might have been such a stay was when Charlie was six. Ten years later Mrs. Chaplin slipped into a psychotic state from which she was never fully to recover. Although Chaplin never, either in his *My Autobiography* or elsewhere, made mention of his mother's periodically drifting in and out of affective contact with him and his brother during his earliest years, the erratic on-again-off-again millionaire theme in *City Lights* can safely be taken as a poignant reflection of such state of affairs. At the same time, of course, it can be presumed to have incorporated memories, however dim, of the inconstant roles during Charlie's infancy of the father and other live-in males, again in terms of the tendency of dreams and other dramatic vehicles to make do with convenient condensations.

Coming back to the theme of oral deprivation woven into the multiple abandonments of Chaplin's early life, other films reflect this in profusion. There is hardly a two-reeler or a later film in which the Little Tramp is not cadging food, stealing food, fighting over food, getting into one kind of trouble or another over food, or showing the pangs of hunger or the bliss of satiety. Most of these scenes are exceedingly funny, but perhaps the most memorable of all is in *The Gold Rush* where Charlie, near starvation in the snowed-in cabin he has come to share with Big Jim, achieves the ultimate in mock gourmet dining. Making the best of Old Mother Hubbard's barren cupboard, he is a study in elegance as the laces and protruding nails of an old shoe he has boiled are made to double for spaghetti and fishbones.

Virtually inseparable from the oral deprivation such scenes reflect are feelings and fantasies of abandonment. This is touchingly portrayed in a later scene in *The Gold Rush* in which the dance hall girls Charlie has invited to dine with him in a borrowed cabin on New Year's Eve cruelly stand him up. Totally crushed, he falls asleep on the table he has set for them and dreams of the dinner coming off in high style after all. It is in this sequence that the celebrated dance of the rolls occurs.

With such direct images of starvation, hurt, and abandonment one might expect some representation, however indirect or symbolic, of the rage that we have come to see as an integral part of this tangle of infantile emotions in the unconscious. (The entrapment of the mother-father in the frozen gear bit in *Modern Times* might be a good example of indirect, or frozen, rage.) Anything like this is not seen in direct form, however, until a restaurant scene in *City Lights,* which went into production two years after *The Gold Rush*; but then it is not Charlie's rage that we see but the almost apoplectic fury of a patron dining alone who, with juices flowing in anticipation of the dinner to come, is victimized by a series of frantic misadventures that prevent Charlie, now a waiter buffeted about in a maelstrom of mishaps, from bringing him his order. In this once again transparent reversal of Charlie's infantile situation (and once again curious gender reversal), the rage, projected onto someone else, is transformed into high comedy, with Charlie merely the helpless instrument of oral deprivation, not the victim.

It is obvious that anything like real rage, real murderous rage, could hardly be expected from the Little Tramp himself. It was not until two decades after *The Gold Rush* that Chaplin, in the guise of a character from which every vestige of the Little Tramp has disappeared, got around to dealing with rage against mother figures in a form that was not almost totally obscured by camouflage of one kind or another; and even then there were so many defenses against the underlying affect that practically nothing remained of the original rage but a hollow simulacrum of the outward appearance of what was plainly a symbolic matricide. In *Monsieur Verdoux,* released in 1947, Chaplin comes on as a Bluebeard who murders his female victims, whom he first marries for their money, without a trace of feeling but purely as a business venture. Any feeling in the film is reserved for Verdoux's crippled real wife, who is less a character than a mannequin cutout symbolizing a mother who cannot go anywhere, paralytically immobilized in a wheelchair as she is. (Another effectually immobilized mother figure, also a structuralized defense against abandonment, was seen in the blind flower girl with whom the Little Tramp becomes involved in *City Lights.*) The one indirect reference to the infantile nursing situation is the fact that the murders are all carried out by providing the victims with some sort of poison to ingest, a method which actually does figure in a certain percentage of orally inspired homicides (and not infrequently, as was pointed out in the last chapter, in the fantasies of *being* poisoned harbored by many paranoid schizophrenics).

The sad part of all this is that Chaplin, as tied up psychologically as was his wife physically in the picture, was unable to breathe real life into this dreary effort, which is often what happens when one's aggressive drives are severely hobbled. The film, trying as hard as it could to be funny, comes off as unfunny, uninteresting, and un-anything that could ever be a credit to its maker.

For a really successful comic treatment of what had to be Chaplin's infantile rage—as defanged in certain respects, however, as Shaw's *Androcles*—we have to turn once again to *The Gold Rush*, released twenty-two years earlier. (In the creative spheres these things rarely follow real-time schedules but are apt to emerge as parts of temporally spread out jigsaw puzzles.) Here the rage, projected outward, bounces back as the fear of being eaten. This happens when Charlie's partner, Big Jim, crazed by a hunger that was scarcely appeased by a boiled shoe, hallucinates Charlie as a chicken and chases him around the cabin with a meal in mind. With what amounts to murderous urges thus fully unleashed (even if projected), this scene *is* funny—except for the moment approaching real horror when Big Jim, realizing that the chicken has been a hallucination, decides to go after his terrorized cabin-mate anyway; but then it is Charlie, not the mother, who is to be cannibalized. This ultimate masochism is completely consonant with the character of the Little Tramp, except in dreams within dreams, as it were, such as the complaisant cow bit in *Modern Times*.

In his private life, Chaplin's dread of abandonment led to exactly that in many of his relationships, where the game of who abandons whom was played out repeatedly with the Little Tramp in his greatest role, that of the abandoned infant. This primary dread was also undoubtedly related, as it often is in the case of abandoned children, to his lifelong habit of keeping two of everything on hand so that he could always have a spare ready in case he ran out of something. He became more secure when, at fifty-four, he married Oona O'Neil, the eighteen year old daughter of playwright Eugene O'Neil, with whom he had eight children. Of the many needs that might have been fulfilled by this fecund relationship, which from all accounts turned out to be a happy one, finally being able symbolically to pin down the sadly unpredictable and elusive mother must almost certainly have been one.

Chapter Nine
The Endless Problem

In the preceding chapters we have seen various ways of coping with the unsatisfied longing for the unpredictable mother or her stand-ins and, as the frustrated and deprived infant experiences it, her equally capricious breast. The main affect that has to be somehow dealt with is unconscious rage. This may not in a strict sense be the identical rage that was aroused in the earliest months of life (as if this original affect, persisting unchanged throughout the years, were somehow stored in some attic of the mind) but an equally powerful one that, evoked by the manifold frustrations, restrictions, and deprivations of everyday life, is unconsciously experienced in terms of the early infantile experience. Few of us, nevertheless, end up thrashing about and screaming, or having visible paroxysms of inarticulate rage (like the restaurant patron in Chaplin's movie who was denied his dinner) when fortune's slings and arrows become particularly outrageous. There are, as we have seen, various mechanisms for the transformation of these mostly unconscious affects into watered down, often symbolic equivalents, or their displacement onto more easily rationalized targets. These, in fact, make up a good part of our everyday behavior, along with destructiveness originating in other stages of development (and triggered by other types of provocation) that might latch onto whatever genetic factors—and there surely are these—that play a role in the predisposition to violence.

All the same, there appears today to be a paucity of ritualized means of dealing with the negative affects universally involved in the mother-child relationship and its later editions. This is the more remarkable in that it is society's business—indeed one of its top priorities—to provide institutionalized outlets for the collective affects of its members. Thus while we might not expect to see Hate-Your-Mother days or bumper stickers, or annual ceremonial burnings in effigy (of Whistler's Mother, say), it should hardly be beyond reason, what with religious and secular examples of the opposite sentiment in such abundance, to expect *something* along these lines to show up in today's societies—something, that is, beyond nursery stories in which wicked witches or big bad wolves get their comeupances, or equivalent fantasies on stage or screen.

One curious exception to this general lack is a custom that exists outside the mainstream of contemporary culture and has in any case never been recognized for what it transparently is. On special settlements on the northernmost island of Japan, Hokkaido, live small groups of a vanishing people, the Ainu, who a century or so ago were still largely aboriginal. Thought to have migrated from Siberia and at one time to have occupied most of Japan prior to the advent of the Japanese, the Ainu seem to have been sidetracked by cultural evolution. Their spoken language is unrelated to any other known speech and they still have no written language. They have, however, preserved a ritual which, in terms of depth psychology, is as valuable a window into the collective mind of humanity as anything in more widely known custom or religion.

The ritual in question, which survived repeated Japanese attempts to ban it and is still sporadically practiced today, is addressed to the mythical ancestress of the Ainu race, a deity named Fuji, which means grandmother, or old woman. It begins with the capture of a bear cub, which is reared for about two years with all the love and care accorded a cherished family member. It is cuddled, petted, and stuffed with food, and may even be suckled by its captor's wife or other women. When it is old enough to require a cage, it is still treated as a member of the family. At the end of this period, however, everything changes. A feast is held at which the lately cherished bear is taken out of its cage and, with expressions of great excitement and joy on the part of the celebrants, taunted, tortured, and brutally strangled by a specially prescribed technique. Here and there a woman— usually the one who has actually reared the cub—sheds a tear and may even make a stylized pretense of trying to strike the bear's tormentors (and executioners); but the ceremony, called *Iomande,* proceeds according to its age-old rules, an integral part of which are the expressions of joy and happiness just mentioned. All the while, high flown speeches are made about having to send the luckless victim back to its ursine ancestors in gratitude for benefits received (food, clothing, etc.). The bear is then flayed and its head cut off and ceremoniously displayed, while under its lifeless snout are tauntingly placed all sorts of delicacies and drinks, again with fulsome expressions of esteem. The rest of the bear is cut open and eaten, and its warm blood smeared over the faces and beards of its late well-wishers. (The women, in accord with an ancient custom of the "hairy Ainu," as these people are sometimes called, have splendid handlebar mustaches tattooed around their lips.) This done, the skull is placed in a row of skulls from similar ceremonies of the past.

The Ainu bear ritual has been conventionally regarded as hunting magic. But this, whatever else it may be, it almost certainly isn't. For one thing, the Ainu have other ceremonies for actual hunts which, like most hunting rituals, involve measures to propitiate the spirit of the hunted animal. From this point of view, to release an animal's spirit by deliberate torture and calculatedly brutal strangulation, followed by taunting it in effigy, as it were, would scarcely seem a successful strategy. Far more likely is the possibility that early missionaries pinned the hunting magic designation on the bear ritual because they were shocked out of their wits by the brutal and bizarre procedure and just didn't know what else to call it. Then, in the days before this sort of thing became a well-recognized pitfall of anthropological technique, they might in all innocence have given the idea to the Ainu, who may since have been dutifully giving it back to their interrogators.

Like many if not most rituals, the Ainu bear ritual has all the earmarks of a charade. But although its central feature, the transformation of affect toward a sacrificial animal from deep caring to its blatant opposite, has no counterpart in magical practices aimed at insuring success in the hunt, there is nothing particularly puzzling about it from the standpoint of depth psychology. It is reminiscent, in fact, of nothing so much as Chaplin's fantasy of an infant's paradise in *Modern Times* in conjunction with the scene in which he is locked into a sadistic feeding machine gone berserk. (The bear is locked into a two-bar neck yoke which is tightened until strangulation occurs. The differing real time order of these fantasies in the Ainu and Chaplin versions should cause no difficulty when it is recognized that the expression of fantasies in dreams and drama, as we have already seen in Shaw's handling of the abandonment sequence in *Pygmalion,* is not bound by considerations of chronological accuracy.) If we now add *Monsieur Verdoux* to the series, the Ainu bear ritual and the Chaplin fantasies may be viewed as psychological equivalents. Both seem patently to suggest the affects and fantasies experienced by a nursling when its expectations and demands, pointedly idealized in both extravaganzas, are, for whatever reason, not met.

In complicated dreams one can sometimes make out the subject being dealt with but not exactly what is being said about that subject. The same is true of rituals and charades. In many rituals, especially those that have been encrusted with layer upon layer of meaning through untold generations, it is often difficult to tell who is playing exactly what role, and especially whether what is being acted out is the remnant of an active or a passive experience. This is certainly the case with the Ainu bear ritual, particularly with its most puzzling part, which is not the strangling or the taunting in effigy of a presumptive symbolic object, but the extraordinary cheerfulness and zest with which this is done, and the fact that the Ainu themselves never tire of stating that the *Iomande* is the happiest and most joyous experience of their lives. If, thus, we are to regard the bear ritual of the Ainu as incorporating both sides of an ambivalent equation we cannot be sure whether it is an expression of ambivalence toward the mother or a caricature of maternal ambivalence toward the child, or—and this is not uncommon in dream and fantasy life—both. Only in the latter cases, however, would the expressions of happiness and joy, which appear to be such an integral part of the ceremony, be at all comprehensible. These could be viewed as exaggerated representations, perhaps in the stylized manner of classical Kabuki drama, of the hard-hearted mother torturing the child and enjoying every minute of it. Similar fantasies, seen in disguised form in nursery tales, are often encountered in paranoid psychotics (and in not a few patients in the deeper stages of analysis).

The question will surely arise, in any case, of why the bear is made the heavy in the puzzling Ainu ritual, and not some other stand-in for the mother. The answer could be that this furry animal, regardless of other meanings it may have in various folklores, or as a totem animal (which, in addition to all the foregoing, it apparently also is in part for the Ainu), is a natural in this role. Anyone who has ever put a child to bed with its ever popular Teddy knows that the bear can be what psychiatrists call a transitional object, which means nothing more than that, like blanket ends, soft furry pieces of any kind, and especially tufts of hair (even the child's own hair), it is a prime substitute for mommy, especially at bed time. Indeed, weaning a child from these security blankets, when they become socially inappropriate, can be more stressful than weaning a child from the breast. (The other side of the picture, of course, is that the bear can, by the same token, become a dangerous and terrifying object in a nightmare.)

To return now to the question of the seeming paucity of socially institutionalized rituals which, like the *Iomande* of the Ainu, might give expression to the latent fear of and hostility to the mother (and by extension to all women) with which so many cultures the world over have been imbued.[1]

The answer to this question, is, alas, all too plain—even though it may require a sort of double-take (especially by the reigning male) to see it: there has never been any special institutionalization of the universal fear and hatred of the perhaps Not-Always-So-Great Mother because *all* society's institutions incorporate a built-in oppression, exploitation, and punishment of mother figures. These things, in a word, are being and mostly always have been lived out—without benefit of special ceremony— in the daily taken-for-granted folkways of humankind from earliest, possibly prehistoric, times, as has been amply documented in the considerable literature on the subject in the past few decades (e.g., de Beauvoir, Bullough, Dinnerstein, Hays). But one need not go back to early Assyrian, Chinese, or Egyptian texts, or the Talmud or the bible itself, or to our extensive records of life in the dark or middle ages in Europe and Asia, to see that history is one long procession of battered women—physically battered (up to quite recently woman bashing was considered a normal male prerogative and even today it is estimated that a battering, sometimes leading to homicide, occurs every fifteen seconds), morally battered (in Aristotle's time women were not even accorded a soul), sexually battered (the idea of rape within marriage has only currently become a viable concept), economically and politically battered. The fact is that the heavily disadvantaged legal, political, social, sexual, familial, and religious position of women is, where indeed not still plentifully in evidence, well within the memory of today's living. One has only to recall that it was not until the twentieth century that women in the United States were given the vote.

Thus, the question "When did you stop beating your mother?" is far from the unanswerable catch-22 trap it appears to be. The answer is that while people as a rule don't beat their mothers directly, they have never stopped doing so collectively, and symbolically in oblique ways such as were seen in cases presented earlier. Even with the advances brought about by today's feminists, however, the average person is as blind to the fact that this endless replay of the infantile situation continues to go on as he is of any of his own ingrained personal habits or tics. As Dorothy Dinnerstein has put it in her powerful plea for other ways of life (*The Mermaid and the Minotaur*), "the hate, fear, loathing, contempt and greed that men express toward woman so pervade the human atmosphere that we breathe them as casually as the city child breathes smog;" and "Most of us are so adapted to this pollution of the everyday social medium—so

desensitized to it, as one becomes desensitized to a steady rumble or stench—
that we can sincerely claim not to be aware of it at all."

There has latterly been a good deal of attention given to the question
of how this sadly unbalanced and inequitable state of affairs came to be,
and also how it is that women themselves came to accept the inferior image
and the submissive role assigned to them. According to followers of the
nineteenth century German scholar J. J. Bachofen, however, this was perhaps not always so. Largely on the basis of age-old myths and the fact that
female deities (or at least objects of worship such as the "Venuses" we met
in Chapter 1) seem to have preceded the male deities in prehistoric times,
Bachofen postulated a state of affairs in which women were the reigning
forces in whatever kinds of group situations came to be when the earliest
humans first emerged from their swamplike existence. Others, who may
not dispute Bachofen's idea of some sort of matriarchy in humankind's past,
feel nevertheless that Bachofen erred in utilizing a too cramped time frame
in which to spell out his hypotheses, and that there were probably as many
matriarchies as there were patriarchies in the vastly extended human past.
Still others hold that matriarchies, if there ever were such, were probably
not true societal structures but merely arrangements governing matters of
nominal descent since the biological role of the male, who was generally
more at risk of abruptly disappearing in the days of the great cave bear and
the saber toothed tiger, had not yet been firmly established.

However this be, the idea of alternating matriarchies and patriarchies
can only push the problem not only of male dominance but of male puni-
tiveness toward women further into the inaccessible reaches of prehistory,
with little to be gained. The question of immediate relevance is not what
kinds of forces were responsible for these things in the distant past but
what could be responsible for the enormous inequalities that have always
existed in historical times and that we can actually get a bead on today.

Present day students of the situation have outdone themselves trying
to come up with causes for the prevailing lopsidedness. For a long time
explanations of a political type held the field, such as the male's superior
strength and, stemming from this, his ability to implement and control the
necessary machinery of subjugation (which, of course, would leave the
question of the origin of matriarchies hanging). Questions such as *why*
the male needed—and still needs—to exercise this machinery, and why
indeed the female has needed to play in with the male's dominating role,
have only lately begun to occupy historians and sociologists.

Various psychological considerations have been called upon to account
for the male's dominating behavior, such as his great underlying fear of

women (who, as is well documented in Hays' *The Dangerous Sex,* have always had a bad press as witches, demons, succubi, and all around bitches), his envy of the female's biological creativity, of her superior intelligence and earthy intuitiveness, to name a few, and not least his need to establish his sexual supremacy in view of the fact, which seems always to have been known, that woman's orgasmic "potency," her capacity to achieve the heights of sexual transport for more sustained and more repeated periods, far exceeded his. Man, it has been claimed, has always felt vulnerable and humiliated by the unhideable fact of his physically all too obvious detumescence.[2]

Granting whatever part factors such as these may have played in the development of woman's secondary role in society, what has not figured prominently in the literature is the aspect of both man's and woman's psychology stressed in the present book, namely, the mother-child relationship in the nursing situation and the powerful affects arising therefrom. This important source of the perennial conflict between the sexes, as well as the manifold transformations and displacements of the affects arising from it, largely escaped being dragged into the fast burgeoning feminist literature until Dinnerstein accorded it a central role in her carefully thought out book. Making liberal use of psychoanalytic insights, she has built a strong case for the basic conditions underlying the oppression of woman arising from the inescapable imperfections of the all encompassing early mother-child relationship. According to her, moreover, both sexes, not just the male, by virtue of both having been part of a situation in which the primary caregiver and in fact breast giver has been a female, have never relinquished the need to take revenge for all the infantile indignities—the deprivations, restrictions, painful absences, and desertions—visited upon them in the earliest years. The fact, furthermore, that woman herself is the hated as well as loved object, and thus harbors an unconscious need to expiate her role as depriver, underlies both woman's legendary masochism and her compliant acceptance of the greatly devalued subordinate role into which she has been cast.

This ongoing situation, at any rate, establishes the parameters within which the insidious and largely taken for granted anti-feminine drama continues to repeat itself in all segments of life. Indeed, the lopsided gender arrangements in the nursery, Dinnerstein holds, are basically responsible for what she terms the "malaise" and (with a nod toward Freud) the discontent of our time.

I am, of course, fundamentally in agreement with this. Nothing could be plainer to the depth psychologist than that everyday life, as we have seen throughout this book, is largely an endless replay, on different stages, of the early infantile situation, and that the outrageous treatment of woman throughout history has been little more than the customization of the infant's rage against her. The overarching need for revenge for past maternal disfavors is, moreover, unconsciously experienced by each generation anew.

There could be, however, an important hidden agenda in all this, if the cases we have seen in earlier chapters—and the endless replication of similar cases in the population at large—are any indication. This is the existence, in members of both sexes, of ineradicable unconscious dread of abandonment by the mother and her unreliable breast. This dread, which has been seen in different guises throughout this book and whose strength and persistence may be encountered in one form or another in every person who has passed through the early nursing experience with less than complete satisfaction—that is to say, everyone, to greater or less degree, cannot be overestimated. Indeed, for all its having escaped major attention thus far, it could conceivably be one of the most influential of the entire complex of factors underlying the oppression and exploitation of women. In fact, the need to *control* the mother, to pin her down and hobble her so that her comings and goings are routinized and rationalized in care of the children, housework, and church—in *Kinder, Küchen und Kirche,* as it has been so aptly expressed in one of the most male dominated societies of recent times—could easily be the one indispensable unconscious need to whose fulfillment all other needs in this situation are subordinate, the need, namely, to rob woman of her independence, to capture her and to make sure that she (the eternal mother, of course) stays captured and can never desert us.

One has only to explore as many cases as the average psychoanalyst does, and in the intensiveness and depth that his method allows, to see the extent to which the unconscious fear of abandonment pervades our lives. This can range, to give a few examples, from marital discord and strife (the invisible presence of infantile affects has always been the bane of the marriage institution, just as sadly unrealistic infantile hopes—and the need to "tie the knot"—have always lured the romantically possessed of both sexes) to over possessiveness of children and friends and a large segment of cases of morbid jealousy (which are not, as some have held, simply overreactions to threatened property rights—people are not driven to homicide or other crimes of passion if their TVs or cars are stolen). The defenses against this fear, moreover, are legion—from innumerable variations of the types of maneuvers we have seen in Descartes, Shaw, Audubon, and hosts of others to compulsive Don Juanism ('No matter, women are a dime a dozen') and the never ending devaluation and depreciation of women ('Who needs them'), to blindly driven acquisitiveness and lust for power, the need for whose actual or symbolic fulfillment is the signature of our neurotically driven culture.

Thus it is, at all events, that through the ages woman has lived in an invisible dungeon and as if bound by the heaviest leg irons. True, individual women, either through their own intelligence and ingenuity or through the good offices of their husbands or lovers, have always enjoyed many of the perks of prestige and power. Their salons, for example, were traditionally breeding grounds of great persons and great events, and there have always been matriarchal women (or crones) whose character, wisdom, and compassion set them apart (if, that is, they escaped being burned as witches). Other women were able to involve themselves in trade and banking, while a few acquired seats on a stock exchange. One thing few of these women ever acquired, however, was the liberty to strike out on their own if it came to leaving their families and the social networks in which they were imbedded. There were no acceptable role models for this, no conceptual tools, no images to facilitate such moves. They could not, in a word, abandon anybody. They could be abandoned, as indeed they were right and left, but turn the tables, except through symbolic gestures, they could not. It was always the men who had the privilege of doing the abandoning and thus reversing the prototypal inequities of the infantile situation. In the middle ages, and in later times also, men could divorce their wives on the flimsiest pretexts (undue frivolity, or lying, for example), while papal indulgences to facilitate this were always available at bargain prices. Women, however, were as hobbled by the law, both civil and ecclesiastical, as criminals. The historian G. G. Coulton, in his *Medieval Panorama,* cites the case of a woman who sued to divorce a brutal husband but who, for her pains, was ordered by the court to "bend the knee, ask forgiveness," and carry on. (Fig. 47, from a medieval woodcut, shows a woman bending the knee.) When a woman was abandoned, moreover, she generally had dismally few options for the future.

The chief symbolic gesture by means of which women in their social captivity could assert the right to an independent selfhood (of sorts) has, apparently, always been that of overt or covert sexual defiance, from the withholding of sexual favors, where possible, to frigidity (genuine or pseudo) or to pre- or post-nuptial infidelity. Woman's defiant sleeping with a stranger on the eve of her marriage—her only answer, perhaps, to man's traditionally bawdy pre-nuptial stag parties—has been well documented

Figure 47
Medieval Wife Beater

by the psychoanalyst Helene Deutsch, in her *The Psychology of Women* (and I can certainly confirm the far from rare occurrence of such behavior from my own observations—as well, also, as the deliberate sowing of doubt as to a child's paternity). It is conceivable that something like this was prevalent enough in earlier times to give rise to the legend (whose actuality is today considered somewhat dubious, however) of the *Jus prima noctis* (or *Droit du seigneur*)—the right of the lord of the manor to avail himself of the virginity (if still in the picture) and in any case the sexual favors of the prospective bride before the husband-to-be gets his chance to do so. Legend or not, the persistent fantasy of such a ritualization of the profound need on the part of woman to assert her sexual independence is in itself significant, if only of the enshrinement in custom and law of the contrary state of affairs.

Returning to the need to capture the wayward mother, its origins may conceivably go back to the fantasies of biting and devouring envisioned by classical psychoanalysis (Chapter 7), particularly by the British psychoanalyst Melanie Klein, in connection with the rage experienced by breast deprived (or simply befuddled) infants. A biological substrate for such affects and fantasies could very well be the most universal of animal functions, the capture and consumption of prey. Giving due consideration to this primal form of oral incorporation would, at least, lend coherence to the fantasies of pinning the mother down, and thus psychologically incorporating her, all too rife in the Shaws, the Hitchcocks, and the Chaplins among us. It would also comfortably accommodate the fears of oral reprisals shown in the work of these and many other artists with the "Jaws" syndrome when their voracious orgies (as they are experienced in the unconscious) bounce back at them. Thus we have *Androcles and the Lion*, *The Birds*, the fantasy of being eaten in Chaplin's *The Gold Rush*, Audubon's dreams and fantasies of being devoured by fearsome animals, the fantasies behind the orally threatening demons seen in innumerable artifacts such as those in figs. 41 through 44 at the end of Chapter 7 and, of course, the similarly threatening females of myth, legend, and nursery tales throughout the ages. That this could manifest itself on a societal level as an unconscious but persistent need to keep the female prey captive and on a tight leash would seem eminently plausible.

As it happens, nowhere better than in the *Iomande* of the Ainu can the interface between such individual and social mechanisms be seen. There was—and very likely still is—among these people one unusual feature in the child rearing situation that could account for the paroxysms of rage to which Ainu infants turn out to be peculiarly entitled. A daily custom of the Ainu is to put their offspring into baskets attached to the roof beams of their huts and leave them there for hours on end no matter how much they scream, which the Ainu hold is good for them. The mother goes about her business, which may take her out of eye and ear shot for considerable periods, oblivious to the clamorous cries of her infant. The screaming sooner or later dies down, of course, but the fantasies of biting and devouring the "not there" mother might then well be at flood tide. Given this unique Ainu twist in the early mother-child situation, at any rate, the value of a ritual such as the *Iomande,* through which the infant has its day in a symbolic reversal of the original nursery situation, is clear.

What now of the future? I must confess that I would have preferred to avoid dealing with such a sixty-four thousand dollar question but, having come this far, I suppose I might as well make a stab at it. Happily, a number of changes for the better have already occurred on various fronts, largely through the efforts of the feminists but partly also, I suspect, as a natural entailment of a general groundswell (a result of Lord knows what mysterious causes) that would seemingly have burst societal shackles on all sides anyway.

However, whether and to what degree the basic unconscious hate and fear of woman can really be mitigated through such changes only the future itself can tell us. Some foresee a greater flexibility in the gender arrangements of the nursery, with men increasingly assuming the status of primary—or at east equal—caregivers, as capable of going far to reverse what remains of the pernicious trends of millennia past. Others see this only as laying the groundwork for men as well as women coming in for all the negative entitlements to which such a position is subject.

Whatever the case, it is not simply a matter of embodying more equitable relationships between the sexes in custom and law—it goes without saying that more can and will be accomplished along these lines—but of changing the powerful unconscious image of the mother and her surrogates. Here we face a situation not unlike the categorical difference between Lamarckian and Mendelian heritability. The first, if it exists at all, is at most cosmetic while the second, based as it is on profound and tenacious features in the life substance itself, and tending to pursue its grand way regardless of direct experience (at best, that is, requiring long ages for favorable mutations to be selected out of the genetic picture), will in all likelihood continue to be a dominant force imposing constraints on the extent to which basic features of the human situation can be altered. What this boils down to is that two different universes are involved, the conscious and the ol' man river unconscious, and these simply do not mix.

Designs and machinations in the former sphere have little effect on the latter.

Thus, it is hardly to be expected that the mother-nursling relationship that has evolved over eons—a relationship which, as stated in the very opening lines of Chapter 1 of this book, "is regulated by a delicate interplay of sight, sound, smell, touch, taste, and still other signals ..."— will easily lend itself to basic alterations without unsuspected penalties of some sort. It could be a case of "the voice is the voice of Jacob [to risk a bit of transsexualism here] but the hands are the hands of Esau." Does that mean that humankind is fated to go on forever with its deep down love and hate of mother figures unaltered? Quite conceivably yes. The fact remains that the tendency toward ambivalence in all relationships and undertakings is an ineradicable hallmark of the human species, as much a permanent fixture of our humaness as anything can be. (Such ambivalence is not native to dogs, by way of contrast, which is a large part of their enduring and endearing charm.) Between that, at any rate, and the fact that it is far more difficult to engage great masses of people on a crusade to change themselves in no matter what direction (loving peace rather than war, say) than idealogues seem ever to imagine, the notion of new gender arrangements in the nursery leading to a more consistently benign unconscious image of mother and her surrogates must remain highly questionable.

If this sounds disconcertingly like the "anatomy is destiny" thesis that feminists loathe most, it may still be possible to bring the unconscious roots of the divided maternal image into the awareness, if not of the masses, which is extremely doubtful, at least of the leaders and manipulators of those societal trends and forces that determine the legal constraints and rewards of our planetary populations. Pending such a development, our inability to do much other than repress and displace the powerful early affects that contribute heavily to most of the bad things that happen on earth will continue to plague us, as it always has.

Somewhat disquieteningly, it seems increasingly to be felt today that this situation may even escalate horrendously, as may now in fact be occurring, what with a frighteningly significant percentage of mothers—the very hub of any society—becoming addicted to a burgeoning variety of substitutes for their own inadequate childhood mothering. Fortunately there are gyroscopic forces in nature, as mysterious as nature herself, that somehow manage—and have always managed—to keep us from going over the brink. If not for these, in fact, humankind might well have self-destructed long ago. Indeed, mental health professionals have always seen instances of unusual strength and fiber arising out of the most horrible childhoods. Frequently, in these cases, there is at least one loving figure, however tenuous, somewhere in the background (but often enough it is the Man of Sorrows, or his equivalent, who has to fill in, which he seems to do beautifully).

These mysterious subterranean forces, to return now to a side of the picture stressed in the opening chapter of this book, could well be related to an aspect of Woman alluded to in a charming bouquet that was tossed to her almost two thousand years ago and which would be exceedingly unlikely to come the way of her male counterpart, no matter how far he may venture into the delights of motherhood-by-proxy in years to come. It is found in the Acts of Thomas, one of the apocrypha that never made it into the official Book (as a result, some think, of anti-feminist politicizing). A woman who had just had the devil driven from her—possibly an early and rejected version of Mary Magdalene—was invited to share in the ensuing Eucharist with the following invocation: "Come, O perfect compassion, Come, O communion of the male, Come, she that knoweth the mysteries of him that is chosen ... Come, the silence that revealeth the great things of the whole greatness, Come, she that manifesteth the hidden things and maketh the unspeakable things plain, the holy dove that beareth the twin young, Come, the hidden mother, Come, she that is manifest in her deeds and giveth joy and rest unto them that are joined to her: Come and communicate with us in this eucharist which we celebrate in thy name and in the love-feast wherein we are gathered at thy calling."[3]

And who knows but what it may have been something not too different from this that early humans, also frightened, were chanting as they passed their Venuses from hand to hand.

Notes

Notes to Chapter 1

1. Linn
2. The graspability of the Venus figurines, curiously, has been insufficiently appreciated by archeologists. The only two instances I know where something like this was postulated was in connection with two stone figures resembling frogs or toads found in Southern California. The first, 6½ inches in length and dated at about 5000 years, was discovered in 1962 and hailed at the time as the oldest work of three dimensional stone art found in the New World. One commentator, noting that the effigy, although showing no signs of having been used as a tool, fit the hand perfectly, wrote: "One has to hold it and feel it and look at it while it moves in one's hands. It seems inconceivable that it was meant to be appreciated otherwise." (Altman.) The second piece, somewhat smaller but with protuberant eyes somewhat like the first piece, was found at the same site five years later. Dated from the same period, it caused great excitement because it had a deliberately made depression on its back into which, wrote the archeologist who discovered it, "one's thumb fits naturally." (Greenwood.) She also wrote, after the symbolic aspect of the first piece's graspability was pointed out (by me in 1964): "This second effigy is even more likely to have been a handcharm than the first one, since its shape, size, weight, and polish all greatly enhance its tactile appeal." One of the symbolic significances with which the frog has been associated from earliest times, as it happens, has been that of abundance and security, which may be presumed to have been derived from the breastlike shape of its protuberant eyes.

Notes to Chapter 2

1. Bowlby
2. Curiously, no one seems ever to have made a similar observation about the game of peekaboo, which surely every infant at one time or another has taken great delight in playing.
3. Descartes did not actually represent these axes as the vertical and horizontal reference lines that today's student has come to know as Cartesian coordinates but smuggled them into the text of his *Géométrie* rather as a tangle of lines and angles (fig. 12) in terms of which he was able to demonstrate a new

151

solution of a problem known to the ancients. The essential innovation of his method lay in his making one line in this tangle the x axis and another line the y axis, to which all other lines, representing distances, could be numerically related.

4. Hademard

Notes to Chapter 3
1. *Sixteen Self-Sketches*
2. Preface to *The Irrational Knot*
3. Ibid.

Notes to Chapter 4
1. A common petroglyphic symbol on Easter Island monoliths, as well as on the main Polynesian islands, is that of a crescent or crescent-shaped ship. Sometimes referred to as a crescent/ship (Van Tilburg), it may well be a condensation of both. Fashioned presumably during a period when ships visited the islands at very infrequent intervals—perhaps only once a year or so, these symbols could very well have expressed the idea that the ships' desolating disappearances over the horizon would, as in the case of the crescent, always be followed sooner or later by joyous reappearances.
2. Paulsen, 1965, Vol. 2.
3. Ibid.
4. Timbs, page 46.
5. Heller, page 78.
6. Ibid., page 66.
7. Ibid., page 67.
8. On the eve of some long needed dental surgery, an elderly patient dreamed of standing alongside of Columbia University's famed statue of Alma Mater while looking up at the equally famed dome of the library behind it. The dome, he noted, had a large crack in it. The meaning of the dream was clear (or as clear as these things ever are): 'There's nothing wrong with my teeth; the trouble is with my dear old Mater's breast.'
9. Lord
10. Ibid.
11. See Stoller for an unusual foot fetish in a child of two with its roots in such an attachment.

Notes to Chapter 5
1. Mellaart
2. Goodenough, Volume 8, p. 41.
3. Dietz
4. Schnier

Note to Chapter 6

Note to Chapter 7
1. *Audubon and His Journals*, Volume 1, page 251.

Notes to Chapter 8

1. Maloney
2. Although *Modern Times* went into production at least a year earlier than *Sabotage*, which was produced in Britain, no evidence of plagiarism on either side has ever come to light. The curious similarity in the two episodes described has to be regarded as one of those intriguing coincidences known to turn up from time to time, such as Newton and Leibniz independently conceiving of the infinitesimal calculus at about the same time, Darwin and Wallace almost simultaneously arriving at the mechanism of natural selection, and God coming up with the idea of creation just moments before the Big Bang.

Notes to Chapter 9

1. Bear skulls arranged in rings and rows, discovered in the early part of this century in prehistoric sites in the Swiss alps and other mountain ranges as far as Siberia, are mutely suggestive of the Ainu bear skull collections.
2. According to an interesting hypothesis put forward by Mary Ann Sherfey, on the other hand, women's insatiable sexuality forced their subjugation when the nomadic hunter-gatherer phase of social evolution gave way to settled communities after the discovery of agriculture and husbandry. Women on the loose simply did not go with the overall needs of such communities which required, among other things, relatively firm parental norms, including a way of establishing paternity.
3. James

Table of Illustrations

Table of Illustrations, continued

Chapter References
For complete entry see Bibliography

Chapter One

Altman, R. 1962
Hayes, H. 1963
Hoffer, W. 1949, pp. 49–55
Kuhn, H. 1956
Lajoux, J-D. ND
Linn, L. 1955
Lewin, B. 1953
Maringer, J. and H-G Bandi, 1953
Meltzoff, A. 1985
Morris, D. 1967
Sander, L. *et. al.* 1979

Chapter Two

Baillet, A. 1691/1970
Bowlby, J. 1969
Descartes, R. 1954, 1955, 1968
Freud, S. 1920/1955
Hademard, J. 1945
Jaspers, K. 1964
Leroy, M. 1929
Lewin, B. 1958
Meyer, B. 1975
Smith, D. 1925
Vrooman, J. 1970

Chapter Three

Baillet, A. 1691/1970
Harris, F. 1931

Heinecke, C. and I. Westheimer, 1965
Henderson, A. 1956
St. John, C. 1951
Shaw, G. B. 1914, 1928, 1931, 1948, 1949, 1975

Chapter Four

Burke, J. 1968
Cook, A. 1954, p. 337
De Chirico, G. 1971
De Polnay, P. 1969
Eliade, M. 1958
George, W. 1964
Goodenough, E. 1953–58
Heller, R. 1972
Lord, J. 1985
Macaulay, D. 1978
Navratil, L. 1969
Paulson, R. 1970, 1974, 1975
Ravenal, C. 1986
Soby, J. 1955
Stoller, R. 1985
Timbs, J. 1872
Van Tilburg, J. and G. Lee, 1987

Chapter Five

Bradley, N. 1965
Dietz, S. 1975
Freud, S. 1910/1957

Chapter References, continued

Goodenough, E. 1956
Mellaart, J. 1962, 1963
O'Neill, J. 1944
Schnier, J. 1952
Vogt, W. 1957, p. 392

Chapter Six
Audubon, J. 1831–39, 1985
Audubon, L. 1869/1894
Audubon, M. 1960
Chancellor, J. 1978
Darwin, C. 1962
DeLatte, C. 1982
Durant, M. and M. Harwood, 1980
Ford, A. 1957, 1964
Harwood, M. and M. Durant, 1985
Heinicke, C., and I. Westheimer, 1965
Herrick, F. 1968
Jacobson, E. 1965
Levine, M. 1982, p. 53
Peterson, R. 1957
Rourke, C. 1936
Wolfenstein, M. 1969

Chapter Seven
Grey, G. 1841/1964
Ions, V. 1984
Lévy-Bruhl, L. 1935
Lewin, B. 1953
Steig, W. 1979
Zimmer, H. 1946

Chapter Eight
Chaplin, C. 1964
Chappelow, A. 1969, 1971
Jacobs, D. 1975
LaValley, A. 1972
Mcdonald, G., M. Conway, M. Ricci, 1965
Maloney, R. 1938
Shaw, G. B. 1886; 1928; 1931; 1948: I; 1949; 1975: I, III, IV; 1983
Silver, A. 1982
Spoto, D. 1983
Robinson, D. 1985

Chapter Nine
Bachofen, J. 1967
Batchelor, J. N.D.
Bordes, F. 1968
Briffault, R. 1959
Brueil, H. and R. Lantier, 1965
Bullough, V. 1973
Coulton, G. 1940
De Beauvoir, S. 1964
Deutsch, H. 1944
Dinnerstein, D. 1976
Frazer, J. 1890/1951
Caylin, W. 1984
Hays, H. 1963, 1964
Hilger, M. 1971
James, M. 1924
Neumann, E. 1972
Sherfey, M. 1970

Attributions

Chapter 1
Fig. 1. Naturhistorisches Museum, Vienna.
Fig. 2. Denver Museum of Natural History cast.
Figs. 3 & 4. Author's cast, courtesy of Dr. Jan Jellinek, Moravske Museum, Brunn, Czechoslovakia.
Fig. 5. Musée des antiquités nationale, St. Germain-en-Laye, France. Photograph: Charles Hurault.
Fig. 6. Musée de l'Homme, Paris.
Fig. 7. Musée des antiquités nationale, St. Germain-en-Laye, France.
Fig. 8. State Historical Museum, Moscow, USSR.
Fig. 9. State Historical Museum, Moscow, USSR.
Fig. 10. "Concretion," Denver Museum of Natural History.

Chapter 2
Fig. 11. Descartes. Musée du Louvre, Paris.
Fig. 12. From Descartes' *Géométrie*.

Chapter 4
Fig. 13. British Museum.
Fig. 14. *Rock Pictures of Europe*. Herbert Kuhn. London: Sidgwick & Jackson, 1956. Munich: Kohlhammer Verlag, 1952.
Fig. 15. *Bogomil Sculpture*. Alojz Benac and Otto Bihalji-Merin. New York: Harcourt, Brace and World. N.D.
Fig. 16. Public domain.
Fig. 17. *Oui* Magazine. Children of God.
Fig. 18. British Museum.
Fig. 19. British Museum.
Fig. 20. Dr. Leo Navratil.
Fig. 21. Nasjonalgalleriet, Oslo.
Fig. 22. Art Institute of Chicago. (Private collector.)
Fig. 23. Art Institute of Chicago.
Fig. 24. Museum of Modern Art, New York, New York. Fig. 21. Tate Gallery, London.

Fig. 26. *Great Moments in Architecture.* David Macaulay. Boston: Houghton Mifflin, 1978.

Chapter 5

Figs. 27, 28. Author's casts, courtesy State Historical Museum, Moscow.

Fig. 29. *Archaeology,* July 1975. Courtesy Dr. Søren Dietz.

Fig. 30. Author's collection.

Fig. 31. Goodenough, E. R. *Jewish Symbols in the Greco-Roman Period.* Vol. 8. New York: Pantheon Books, 1953–1958.

Fig. 32. *Saturday Evening Post,* Curtis Publishing Company.

Fig. 33. From the color original of Lester Kraus. *Cavalier* Magazine, December 1965.

Chapter 7

Fig. 34. Source unknown. From Neumann, Erich. *The Great Mother: an Analysis of the Archetype.* Bollingen Series 47. Princeton, New Jersey: Princeton University Press, 1974.

Fig. 35. St. Pierre de Chauvigny. From Bush, Harold and Lohse, Bernd. *Romanesque Europe* Macmillan, 1960.

Fig. 36. Eugene Mihaesco, *Time* Magazine, June 23, 1986.

Fig. 37. Exhibition Delegation, "Art Treasures from Japan," 1958, from Janson, H. W. and Janson, D. J. eds., *Key Monuments in the History of Art: A Visual Survey.* New York: Abrams, 1959.

Fig. 38. Source lost in the author's files.

Fig. 39. Lorenz, in *The New Yorker,* February 4, 1991.

Fig. 40. Author's ownership.

Fig. 41. John Dempsey, *Playboy* Magazine, September 1968.

Fig. 42. *Australia—Aboriginal Paintings: Arnhem Land.* Greenwich, Connecticut: New York Graphic Society. Unesco Art Series, 1954.

Fig. 43. William P. Hoest, in *Parade* Magazine.

Fig. 44. *Indian Mythology.* Veronica Ions. New York: Peter Bedrick Books. Courtesy Hamlyn Publishing, Twickenham, Middlesex, England.

Fig. 45, 46. William Steig, in *William Steig Drawings.* New York: Farrar, Straus & Giroux, 1979.

Chapter 9

Fig. 47. From G. G. Coulton, *Medical Panorama.* Cambridge: Cambridge University Press, 1940.

Bibliography

Chapter 1

Altman, Ralph C. A note on the effigy from the Browne Site. *The Masterkey,* 36:7, 38, 1962.

Eisenbud, Jule. A recently found carving as a breast symbol. *American Anthropologist,* 66, 1, 1964, 141–147.

Hayes, H. R. *In The Beginnings: Early Man and His Gods.* New York: G.P. Putnam's Sons, 1963.

Hoffer, Willi. Mouth, Hand and Ego Integration. In *The Psychoanalytic Study of the Child,* Vol. III–IV. New York: International Universities Press, 1949, 49–55.

Kuhn, Herbert. *Rock Pictures of Europe.* London: Sidgwick & Jackson, 1956.

Lajoux, Jean-Dominique. *The Rock Paintings of Tassili.* Cleveland, Ohio: World Publishing Co., N.D.

Linn, Louis. Some Developmental Aspects of the Body Image. *International Journal of Psycho-Analysis,* 36, 1955, 36–42.

Lewin, Bertram D. Reconsideration of the Dream Screen. *The Psychoanalytic Quarterly.* Vol. 22, No. 2, 1953, 174–199.

Maringer, Johannes and Bandi, Hans-Georg. *Art in the Ice Age.* New York: Frederick A. Praeger, 1953.

Meltzoff, Andrew N. The Roots of Social and Cognitive Development: Models of Man's Original Nature. In *Social Perception in Infants.* Eds. Field, Tiffany, and Fox, Nathan. Norwood, New Jersey: Ablex Publishing Corporation, 1985.

Morris, Desmond. *The Naked Ape.* New York: McGraw-Hill, 1967.

Sander, Louis W. et al. Change in Infant and Caregiver Variables over the First Two Months of Life: Integration of Action in Early Development. In E. Thoman (ed.) *Origin of the Infant's Social Responsiveness.* New Jersey: Lawrence Erlbaum Associates, Inc., 1979.

Chapter 2

Baillet, Adrien. *La Vie de Monsieur Descartes.* Geneva: Slatkine Reprints, 1691/1970.

Bowlby, John. *Attachment and Loss.* New York: Basic Books, 1969.

Descartes, René. *Geometry* (tr. D. E. Smith and M. L. Latham). New York: Dover, 1954.

Descartes, René. The Pinciples of Philosophy. In *Philosophical Works of Descartes* (tr. E. S. Haldane and G.R.T. Ross), Vol. 1. New York: Dover, 1955.

Descartes, René. *Discourse on Method and the Meditations* (tr. F. E. Sutcliffe). Baltimore: Penguin Books, 1968.

Freud, Sigmund. *Beyond the Pleasure Principle.* Complete Psychological Works of Sigmund Freud (tr. James Strachey et al.), Vol. 18. London: Hogarth Press, 1920.

Hademard, J. *The Psychology of Invention in the Mathematical Field.* New York: Dover, 1945.

Jaspers, Karl. *Three Essays: Leonardo, Descartes, Max Weber.* New York: Harcourt, Brace, 1964.

Leroy, M. *Descartes: le philosophe au masque.* 2 vols. Paris: Rieder, 1929.

Lewin, Bertram D. *Dreams and th Uses of Regression.* New York: International Universities Press, 1958.

Meyer, Bernard. *Joseph Conrad.* Princeton: Princeton University Press, 1975.

Smith, D. E. *History of Mathematics.* Vol. 2. Boston: Ginn, 1925.

Vrooman, J. R. *René Descartes: A Biography.* New York: Putnam, 1970.

Chapter 3

Baillet, Adrien. *La Vie de Monsieur Descartes.* Geneva: Slatkine Reprints, 1691/1970.

Harris, Frank. *Bernard Shaw.* New York: Simon & Schuster, 1931.

Heinecke, Christoph M. and Westheimer, Ilse J. *Brief Separations.* New York: International Universities Press, 1965.

Henderson, Archibald. *George Bernard Shaw: Man of the Century.* New York: Appleton-Century-Crofts, 1956.

St. John, C. (ed.) *Ellen Terry and Bernard Shaw: A Correspondence.* New York: Putnam.

Shaw, Bernard. Pygmalion. In *Selected Plays,* Vol. I. New York: Dodd, Mead & Company 1948.

Shaw, G. B. *Immaturity.* London: Constable, 1931.

Shaw, G. B. *Sixteen Self-Sketches.* New York: Dodd, Mead, 1949.

Shaw, G. B. *The Irrational Knot.* London: Constable, 1914.

Chapter 4

Burke, Joseph and Caldwell, Colin. *Hogarth: The Complete Engravings.* London: Thames and Hudson, 1968.

Cook, A. B. *Zeus: A Study in Ancient Religion,* Vol. 2. New York: Biblo and Tannen, 1964. Plate XXIV, 2, 337.

De Chirico, Giorgio. *Memoirs.* Miami, Florida: University of Miami Press, 1971.

De Polnay, Peter. *Enfant Terrible: The Life and Work of Maurice Utrillo.* New York: Morrow, 1969.

Eliade, Mircea. *Patterns in Comparative Religion.* New York: Sheed & Ward, 1958.

George, Waldemar. *Utrillo.* Greenwich, Connecticut: New York Graphic Society, 1964.

Goodenough, Erwin R. *Jewish Symbols in the Greco-Roman Period,* Vols. I–VII. New York: Pantheon Books, Inc., 1953–1958.

Heller, Reinhold. *The Art of Edvard Munch: The Scream.* New York: Viking Press, 1972.

Lord, James. *Giacometti: a Biography.* New York: Farrar, Straus & Giroux, 1985.

Macaulay, David. *Great Moments in Architecture.* Boston: Houghton Mifflin Co., 1978.

Navratil, Leo. *Krankheitsverlauf und Zeichnung (im Himblick auf die Kreativitat. Confin. Psychiat.* 12:28–39, 1969.

Paulson, Ronald. *Hogarth: His Life, Art and Times.* Abridged Ed. New Haven: Yale University Press, 1974.

Paulson, Ronald. *The Art of Hogarth.* London: Phaidon, 1975.

Paulson, Ronald, compiler and commentator. *Hogarth's Graphic Works.* Revised edition. New Haven: Yale University Press, 1970.

Ravenal, Carol M. Three Faces of Mother: Madonna, Martyr, Medusa in the Art of Edvard Munch. *Journal of Psychohistory,* 13, 4, Spring 1986, 371–412.

Timbs, John. *Anecdote Lives of William Hogarth, Sir Joshua Reynolds, Thomas Gainsborough, Henry Fuseli, Sir Thomas Lawrence, and J. M.W. Turner.* London: Richard Bentley, 1872.

Van Tilburg, Joanne and Lee, Georgia. Symbolic Stratigraphy: Rock Art and the Monolithic Statues of Easter Island. *World Archeology.* Vol. 19, No. 2, 1987, 133–149.

Chapter 5

Bradley, Noel. The Vulture as Mother Symbol: A Note on Freud's Leonardo. *American Imago,* 22, 1965.

Dietz, Søren. A Bronze Age Tumulus Cemetery in Asine, Southern Greece. *Archaeology,* 28, 1975, 157–163.

Freud, Sigmund. *Leonardo da Vinci and a Memory of his Childhood.* Complete Psychological Works of Sigumnd Freud. Standard Edition (trans. James Strachey et al.), Vol. 11. London: Hogarth Press, 1957.

Goodenough, Erwin C. *Jewish Symbols in the Greco-Roman Period.* Vols. 5, 8. New York: Pantheon Books, Inc., 1956.

Mellaart, James. Deities and Shrines of Neolithic Anatolia: Excavations at Catal Huyuk, 1962. *Archaeology,* 16, 1963, 29–38.

O'Neill, John J. *Prodigal Genius: The Life of Nikola Tesla.* New York: Ives Washburn, 1944.

Schnier, Jacques. The Symbolic Bird in Medieval and Renaissance Art. *American Imago,* IX, 1952, 1–29.

Vogt, William. *Birdwatcher's Anthology* (Ed. Roger T. Peterson). New York: Harcourt Brace, 1957, 392.

Chapter 6

Audubon, John James. *The Birds of America.* New York: Macmillan, 1985.

Audubon, John James. *Ornithological Biography; or, An Account of the Habits of the Birds of the United States of America; Accompanied by the Descriptions of the Objects Represented in the Work Entitled "The Birds of America," and Interspersed with Delineations of American Scenery and Manners.* 5 vols. Edinburgh: A. Black, 1831–39.

Audubon, Lucy, ed. *The Life of Audubon the Naturalist.* New York: Putnam's, 1869/1894.

Audubon, Maria R., ed. *Audubon and his Journals.* 2 vols. New York: Dover Publications, 1960.

Chancellor, John. *Aubudon.* New York: Viking, 1978.

Darwin, Charles. *The Voyage of the Beagle.* New York: Doubleday Anchor, 1962.

DeLatte, Carolyn E. *Lucy Audubon: A Biography.* Baton Rouge: Louisiana State University Press, 1982.

Durant, Mary and Harwood, Michael. *On the Road with John James Audubon.* New York: Dodd, Mead & Company, 1980.

Ford, Alice. *John James Audubon.* Norman, Oklahoma: University of Oklahoma Press, 1964.

Ford, Alice, ed. *Bird Biographies of John James Audubon.* New York: 1957.

Harwood, Michael and Durant, Mary. In search of the Real Mr. Audubon. *Audubon,* May 1985, 58–119.

Herrick, Francis Hobart. *Audubon, The Naturalist: A History of his Life and Time.* 2 vols. New York: Dover, 1968.

Heinicke, C. M. and Westheimer, I. J. *Brief Separations.* New York: International Universities Press, 1965.

Jacobson, Edith. The Return of the Lost Parent. In *Drives, Affects and Behavior,* Vol. 2. Ed. Max Schur. New York: International Universities Press, 1965, 193–211.

Levine, Martin. An interview with Roger Tory Peterson. *Book Digest,* March 1982, 53.

Peterson, Roger Tory, ed. *The Bird Watcher's Anthology.* New York: Harcourt, Brace and Company, 1957.

Rourke, Constance. *Audubon.* New York: Harcourt Brace, 1936.

Wolfenstein. Loss, Rage, and Repetition. *The Psychoanalytic Study of the Child,* 24, 1969. New York: International Universities Press, 432–460.

Chapter 7

Ions, Veronica. *Indian Mythology.* New York: Peter Bedrick Books, 1984.

Levy-Bruhl, Lucien. *Primitives and the Supernatural.* New York: E. P. Dutton and Company, 1935.

Lewin, Bertram D. Reconsideration of the Dream Screen. *The Psychoanalytic Quarterly.* Vol, 22, No. 2, 1953, 174–199.

Steig, William. *William Steig Drawings.* New York: Farrar, Straus & Giroux, 1979.

Zimmer, Heinrich. Myths and symbols in Indian Art. Ed. Joseph Campbell. Bollingen Series VI. Princeton: Princeton University Press; also New York: Pantheon Books, 1946.

Chapter 8

Chaplin, Charles. *My Autobiography.* New York: Simon & Schuster, 1964.

Chappelow, Allan. *Shaw—The Chucker-Out.* London: 1969; New York: AMS Press, 1971.

Jacobs, David. *The Chaplin Movies and Charlie.* New York: Harper & Row, 1975.
McDonald, Gerald D., Conway, Michael, Ricci, Mark, Eds. *The Films of Charlie Chaplin.* New York: Bonanza Books, 1965.
Maloney, Russell. *And What Happened Next? A Profile of Alfred Hitchcock. New Yorker.* Sept. 10, 1938.
Silver, Arnold. *Bernard Shaw: The Darker Side.* Stanford, California: Stanford University Press, 1982.
Shaw, Bernard. Androcles and the Lion. In *Bernard Shaw: Collected Plays with their Prefaces.* New York: Dodd, Mead & Company, 1975, Volume IV.
Shaw, Bernard. Candida. In *Bernard Shaw: Collected Plays with their Prefaces.* New York: Dodd, Mead & Company, 1975, Volume I.
Shaw, Bernard. Major Barbara. In *Bernard Shaw: Collected Plays and their Prefaces.* New York: Dodd, Mead & Company, 1975, Volume III.
Shaw, Bernard. Pygmalion. In *Bernard Shaw: Collected Plays and their Prefaces.* New York: Dodd, Mead & Company, 1975, Volume IV.
Shaw, Bernard. *The Intelligent Woman's Guide to Socialism and Capitalism.* New York: Brentano's, 1928.
Shaw, G. B. *Cashel Byron's Profession.* London: Scott, 1886.
Shaw, G. B. *Immaturity.* London: Constable, 1931.
Shaw, G. B. *Sixteen Self-Sketches.* New York: Dodd, Mead, 1949.
Spoto, Donald. *The Dark Side of Genius: The Life of Alfred Hitchcock.* Boston: Little, Brown, 1983.
Robinson, David. *Chaplin, His Life and Art.* New York: McGraw Hill, 1985.
LaValley, Albert J., ed. *Focus on Hitchcock.* Englewood Cliffs, NJ: Prentice-Hall, 1972.

Chapter 9
Bachofen, Johann Jakob. *Myth, Religion, and Mother Right.* Selected writings of J. J.Bochofen. Translated by Ralph Mannheim. Bollingen Series LXXXIV. Princeton, NJ: Princeton University Press, 1967.
Batchelor, John. *The Ainu and their Folklore.* New York: Krishna, N.D.
Beauvoir, Simone de. *The Second Sex.* New York: Knopf, 1964.
Bordes, Francois. *The Old Stone Age.* New York: McGraw-Hill, 1968.
Briffault, Robert. *The Mothers.* Abr. Ed. New York and London: George Allen & Unwin, 1959.
Brueil, Henri and Lantier, Raymond. *The Men of the Old Stone Age.* London: C. G. Harrap, 1965.
Bullough, Vern L. *The Subordinate Sex: A History of Attitudes Toward Women.* Urbana: University of Illinois Press, 1973.
Coulton, G. G. *Medieval Panorama.* Cambridge: Cambridge University Press, 1940.
Deutsche, Helene. *The Psychology of Women,* New York, Grune and Stratton, 1944.
Dinnerstein, Dorothy. *The Mermaid and the Minotaur: Sexual Arrangements and Human Malaise.* New York: Harper & Row, 1976.
Frazer, James George. *The Golden Bough.* Two volumes. Parts I–VIII reprinted. New York: Macmillan, 1951 (1890).

Gaylin, Willard. *The Rage Within: Anger in Everyday Life.* New York: Simon & Shuster, 1984.

Hays, H. R. *In The Beginnings: Early Man and His Gods.* New York: G. P. Putnam's Sons, 1963.

Hays, H. R. *The Dangerous Sex: The Myth of Feminine Evil.* New York: Putnam's, 1964.

Hilger, M. Inez. *Together with the Ainu, a Vanishing People.* Norman, Oklahoma: University of Oklahoma Press, 1971.

James, M. R. *The Apocryphal New Testament.* Oxford: The Clarendon Press, 1924.

Neumann, Eric. *The Great Mother: An Analysis of the Archetype.* Bollingen Paperback Edition. Princeton, NJ: Princeton University Press, 1972.

Sherfey, Mary Ann. In *Sisterhood is Powerful: An Anthology of Writings from the Women's Liberation Movement.* Ed. by Robin Morgan. New York: Random House, 1970.

Walker, Barbara. *The Crone: Woman of Age, Wisdom and Power.* New York: Harper and Row, 1985.

Index by Name

Index by Subject

Abandoned child category widened
  to meaninglessness, 64
Abandonment, by men, 145
Abandonment, by mother or care-
  taker, 30, 34, 35. *See also* Separation
  Audubon, 97
  Chaplin, 134
  confusion of budding self and
    object, 104
  controlling space, 39–40, 41
  Descartes, 39
  Shaw, 39
  suppression of attachment to
    those who abandon, 30–31
  by women in reality, 145
Abandonment, fear of, xii, 39–40,
  59
  acquisitiveness and lust for power,
    145
  ambivalence toward mother, xii
  defenses vs., 144
  devaluation and depreciation of
    women, 145
  Don Juanism, 145
  pervasiveness in life, 144
  reflections in perspective, 59
Actors as "cattle" (Hitchcock), 122
Ainu, 138, 139, 140, 147
Ambivalence
  in Audubon, 98

in Hitchcock, 124–25
  to mother, women, xii, 115, 117
  in Shaw, 117
  to violence, Shaw, 118
Anti-Aristotelian device, 124
Archetypal female
  attenuated image in work of
    William Steig, 115
  starkest form, Kali (Hindu god-
    dess), 115
Attachment to mother, pathological:
  Hitchcock, 122
Audubon, John James, 89–100
  biographical puzzles, 89–90,
    93–95, 97, 99
  birds, obsession with, 89–90
  denial of stepmother's death, 99
  inner need for revenge upon aban-
    doning mother, 99
  love of shooting, killing wildlife,
    90, 92
  senile regression to ill-nurtured
    childhood, 100
Audubon Society, irony of name, 90

Biographers' ignoring sorrows of
  infancy and childhood, 64
Bird-breast equation, 74–75, 81
  bird watching as mechanism for
    fantasied control of mother, 84
  clinical usefulness, 81